JN025078

Stories of Pioneers

Paths to Reading through Grammar

SHOHAKUSHA

はじめに

英文法を味方につけよう

　英語が出来れば楽しいかも……と思う人は少なくないでしょう。洋楽、映画やゲームなどのエンターテイメントに限らず、コロナ禍によって急速に拡大した国内外のオンライン・コミュニケーションの世界でも、英語の実用価値は高まる一方です。洋書や専門の論文の解読や海外旅行となれば、今やこの言語の習得は必須と言っても過言ではありません。

　しかし学習者を悩ませる最大の要因の一つは、英文法規則の複雑さにあるのではないでしょうか。語学好きで英文法を主に学ぶ人もいますが、ほとんどの学生のみなさんは英語の勉強以外に多くのマルチタスクを抱えています。簡素化された文法体系をできるだけ効率よく、短期間で習得しましょう。

　本書は一般的な英語のルールについて、最低限これだけを押さえようという趣旨で作られました。文法規則を学びつつ、実用英会話や面白い読み物を満載したこの1冊を集中的に学習しさえすれば、英文法という大樹の太い幹が脳内で確実に育ち始めます。それはのちに枝葉を増やし、あなたの人生に必ず豊かな実りをもたらしてくれるでしょう。

著者記す

CONTENTS

英語の文

Grammar **Check**

次の英文を見てみましょう。

> My friend Ken will hold a party that is open to all. Are you free
> tonight? Come on! What a chance to meet people!

● 語・句・節

文（Sentence）を構成する最小の単位を「語（Word）」といいます。

My, friend, Ken, will, hold…

二つ以上の語がまとまって意味を表す場合、次の二通りがあります。

句 (phrase)	My friend Ken, a party, come on など …主語＋動詞を含まないもの
節 (clause)	that is open to all…主語＋動詞を含むもの

● 文の要素と修飾語

最初の英文は大きく二つに分けることができます。

┌─ 主部 (Subject) ─┐

My friend Ken **will hold a party that is open to all.**

└──────── 述部 (Predicate) ────────┘

主部の中心となるのが名詞（名詞相当語句）で「主語」、述部の中心となるのが動詞（動詞句）で「述語動詞」といいます。

📙 文の種類

意味内容から次の 4 つに分類されます。

普通に事実を述べている文…「平叙文」
My friend Ken will hold a party that is open to all.

相手に何かを尋ねる文…「疑問文」
Are you free tonight?

何かを命じたり提案したりする文…「命令文」
Come on!

感動を表す文…「感嘆文」(How か What)
What a chance to meet people!

Applying Grammar

 Audio 02

1 〜 3 の英文を日本語に訳し、4 〜 6 の日本語の意味に合うように (　　) 内に適語を入れましょう。

1. My niece, who has a little daughter, is in hospital.

   _____

2. The puppy kept barking all night so that we couldn't sleep.

   _____

3. You saw the older man walking around yesterday, didn't you?

   _____

4. マネージャーは話し合いのため私たちに部屋を片付けてほしいと言った。

   The manager (　　　　　) us to clean the room for the meeting.

5. 私たちは先週、研究室でその外国人留学生たちに会った。

   We (　　　　　) the foreign students at our laboratory last week.

6. そんなこと言ってくれるなんてあなたはなんて親切なんだ！

   (　　　　　) kind of you to say such a thing!

Understanding English in Conversation

次の会話を読んで問いに答えましょう。

Chuck Yeager © U.S. Air Force photo

Dennis: Shunji, look at this photo. Do you know this man?

Shunji: No, ⬚. But he looks cool! Who is he?

Dennis: Chuck Yeager. He was an American pilot. In 1947, on October 14, Yeager broke "the sound barrier." He became
5   the first person in the world to fly faster than the speed of sound.

Shunji: What does it mean to fly faster than the speed of sound?

Dennis: The speed of sound, known as "Mach 1," is the time it takes for a sound wave to travel from one place to another.

10 **Shunji:** I can't believe a human being could fly that fast. Was it a once-in-a-lifetime adventure for him?

Dennis: No. He did it many times. Believe it or not, Chuck did the same thing in [   ], exactly 50 years after his first flight. On the same day, at the same time.

15 **Shunji:** Really? So, he kept on returning to that supersonic world no human being before him had experienced. Amazing!

 Notes ℓ.3 Chuck Yeager: 1923-2020   ℓ.8 Mach 1: 音速 (≒ 1225 km/h)
ℓ.11 once-in-a-lifetime: 生涯一度の   ℓ.15 supersonic: 超音速の

6

問1 2人は何について話していますか？　A) ～ D) の選択肢の中から選びましょう。

A) 新しく始まる宇宙工学の講義内容

B) 人類初の太平洋無着陸横断の話

C) 航空史に残る英雄

D) パイロット免許を取る方法について

答：☐

問2 各々適切な答を A) ～ D) の選択肢の中から選びましょう。

1. ☐ に入る適切な応答はどれですか？

A) I like the pilot, too

B) I've never seen him

C) I don't have a camera

D) I know him well

2. [　] に入るのは次のどれですか？

A) 1947　　B) 1957　　C) 1997　　D) 2017

3. 本文の内容として正しいものはどれですか？

A) This pilot was the first to exceed the speed of sound.

B) Humans cannot fly at supersonic speeds repeatedly.

C) Shunji knows well about Chuck Yeager.

D) Dennis and Shunji want to fly their plane.

答：| 1 | | 2 | | 3 | |

Understanding English through Reading

🔊 Audio 04

次の英文を読んで、問いに答えましょう。

In 1889, two women began an incredible race around the world when there were still no airplanes. Nellie Bly was
5　a newspaper reporter in New York. She had read Jules Verne's novel *Around the World in 80 Days* and decided

Nellie Bly and Elizabeth Bisland @ Library of Congress, AN

to attempt the world record set by its fictional hero, Phileas Fogg.

10　　Bly successfully persuaded her boss, who was opposed to women traveling alone. On November 14, 1889, Nellie Bly chose only one dress and hurriedly boarded a ship bound for London, taking off on her round-the-world journey.

　　Another woman, Elizabeth Bisland, was a journalist in the
15　same city. Bisland was reluctant at first, but her boss, hoping for magazine sales, encouraged her. Bisland jumped on a ship bound for Japan, starting across the Pacific Ocean a few hours after Bly left in the opposite direction. Both knew they were in a race against time.

20　　In France, however, Bly made a detour to visit Jules Verne. Finally, on January 25, 1890, Bly completed her record-breaking 72-day, six-hour journey. More than 10,000 people gathered at the train station in Jersey City to welcome her back.

　　Bly's success was reported in American and European
25　newspapers. Bisland, on the other hand, completed her journey in 76 days and 16 hours. They were brave women who crossed four oceans and two continents by boat, train, and on horseback.

Notes *ℓℓ*.6-7 Jules Verne：ジュール・ヴェルヌ（フランスの小説家）　*ℓℓ*.7-8 *Around the World in 80 Days*：『八十日間世界一周』　*ℓ*.9 fictional：架空の　*ℓ*.20 make a detour：寄り道をする

問1 下線部を日本語に訳しましょう。

_____

_____

問2 ネリー・ブライが世界一周旅行に挑戦した理由は何ですか？　日本語で答えましょう。

_____

_____

問3 二人の世界記録への挑戦で異なる点は何ですか？　日本語で答えましょう。

_____

_____

問4 1 ～ 5の英文が本文の内容と一致していれば**T**を、そうでなければ**F**を○で囲みましょう。

1. Phileas Fogg is famous for being the first real person to travel around the world in 80 days. (T or F)

2. In 1889, newspaper and magazine companies did not let women work as journalists. (T or F)

3. Both women traveled in different directions and returned on the same day. (T or F)

4. In the end, Bly and Bisland were able to complete their travels in less than 80 days. (T or F)

5. The woman who met Jules Verne was welcomed back by many people at the train station. (T or F)

UNIT 2　8 品詞とその働き

Grammar **Check**

次の英文を見てみましょう。

> Ken got everything he needed from his grocery shop and cooked dinner for the party by himself. Wow!

8つの品詞 (Eight Parts of Speech)

Unit 1 で学んだように、文の中では、それぞれの語が様々な役割を果たします。その役割を大きく分けると8つの働きに分類されます。

1	名詞 (noun)	Ken, grocery shop, dinner	物の名前
2	代名詞 (pronoun)	everything, he, his, himself	名詞の代わり
3	動詞 (verb)	got, needed, cooked	動きや状態を表す
4	形容詞 (adjective)	all	名詞を修飾する
5	副詞 (adverb)	alone	動詞などを修飾する
6	前置詞 (preposition)	from, for, by	名詞の前に置かれる
7	接続詞 (conjunction)	and	語や文を繋ぐ働き
8	間投詞 (interjection)	wow	強い感情をあらわす

8品詞を間違いなくスラスラと挙げることは意外に難しいのです。
上記1～8の太字部分を「8品詞語呂合わせ」で簡単に覚えましょう！

名代 (みょうだい：代理人の事) 動いて敬服、善に接し感嘆
1 2　　　3　　4　　5　　6　　7　　8
名・代名詞　動詞　形容詞　副詞　前置詞　接続詞　間投詞

＊文法用語には、「詞」とつくものが他にもあります。

> 助動詞　　⇒　動詞の仲間
> 準動詞　　⇒　動詞から派生したもの
> 冠詞、数詞 ⇒　形容詞の仲間

 間投詞

思わず口から出る言葉で、「感嘆詞」ともいいます。

> Dear me!（おやまあ）　　Whoops!（しまった）　　My God!（ああ！）　等

Applying Grammar

🔊 Audio 05

1 ～ 6 の下線部の品詞を答えましょう。

1. Lily put her hand in the bathtub.

   Lily ⇒ _____　hand ⇒ _____　bathtub ⇒ _____

2. Mao entered the famous university of music.

   entered ⇒ _____　famous ⇒ _____

3. The girl is at the top of all classes.

   the ⇒ _____　of ⇒ _____

4. Aoi always walks or swims in the morning.

   always ⇒ _____　or ⇒ _____

5. Oh, are you in his class?

   Oh ⇒ _____　you ⇒ _____

6. They didn't know the wealthy man.

   They ⇒ _____　wealthy ⇒ _____

Understanding English in Conversation

次の会話を読んで問いに答えましょう。

Mayu: Look at this beautiful (1) of various landscapes.

Kenta: ① Oh, this is Shuri Castle! It ② became a World Heritage Site in 2000. I'm ③ from Okinawa, so I was shocked by the news of the fire in 2019.

5 **Mayu:** According to the caption, ④ it was the palace of the Ryukyu Kingdom between 1429 and 1879. It was destroyed during World War II, ⑤ but later, the ⑥ main buildings of the central castle and the surrounding walls were rebuilt.

Kenta: I hope it will come back to life like the legendary phoenix.

10 **Mayu:** Yes! Many people have already donated money for its reconstruction.

Kenta: Some ⑦ researchers are attempting a 3D digital reconst-ruction of the castle using tens of thousands of photos sent in by the public. I lived ⑧ near the castle and sent photos I

15 took in high school.

Notes ℓ.2 Shuri: 首里（沖縄県那覇市の一地域） ℓℓ.2-3 World Heritage Site: 世界遺産 ℓ.5 caption: （短い）説明文 ℓℓ.5-6 The Ryukyu Kingdom: 琉球王国 ℓ.9 legendary phoenix: （火中から蘇る）伝説の不死鳥 ℓ.11 reconstruction: 再建 ℓ.12 3D digital (form): ３次元の製品を造形する機器を用いて作成された立体物や像

問1 下線部①〜⑧の品詞を答えましょう。

①＿＿＿＿＿＿＿　②＿＿＿＿＿＿＿　③＿＿＿＿＿＿＿　④＿＿＿＿＿＿＿

⑤＿＿＿＿＿＿＿　⑥＿＿＿＿＿＿＿　⑦＿＿＿＿＿＿＿　⑧＿＿＿＿＿＿＿

問2 適切な答を A) 〜 D) の中から選びましょう。

1. （ 1 ）に入る適切な名詞はどれですか？

A) chart

B) map

C) storybook

D) photobook

2. 〜〜〜〜 線部分の句はどれですか？

A) 動詞句　　**B)** 名詞句　　**C)** 形容詞句　　**D)** 副詞句

3. 本文の内容として正しいものはどれですか？

A) Shuri Castle survived wars, keeping its original appearance.

B) Kenta has known the castle since he was a boy.

C) Mayu doesn't know if any money was raised for the castle.

D) Rebuilding Shuri Castle will cost a lot, so there is no hope for it.

答：	1		2		3	

Understanding English through Reading

次の英文を読んで、問いに答えましょう。

In Spain, there is an unusual cathedral. It was built by a retired monk. The Cathedral of Justo is a majestic building with 12 towers, standing on a 4,700-square-meter site. It is visible from a distance. The pillars supporting the central dome are made from stacked oil

5　drums and the windows are made of pieces of colored glass glued together. In short, the materials used were mainly scrap and waste from other construction sites, so the building truly demonstrates the spirit of recycling.

　　The builder was Justo Gallego Martínez. He was forced to

10　leave a Trappist monastery in his mid-30s because of infectious tuberculosis. He then began his project of building a cathedral on his land. Justo started to collect various materials that had been thrown away. Since

15　then, for more than 60 years, he essentially worked on his own to build his cathedral. He had never formally studied architecture, and the work was

20　carried out without blueprints. He made money by selling or renting portions of his inherited farmland. Justo was not entirely alone. He had some people who volunteered to help him. But basically, he built it as he liked. Donations from supporters and visitors also helped him. Though Justo died in November 2021 at

25　the age of 96, his work has not been lost. Even now, his supporters are working on completing the cathedral on his behalf.

 Notes　ℓ.2 Cathedral of Justo: フスト大聖堂　ℓ.9 Justo Gallego Martínez: フスト・ガジェ ゴ・マルティネス（人名）　ℓ.10 Trappist monastery: トラピスト修道院　ℓ.11 tuberculosis: 結核　ℓ.20 blueprint: 設計図　ℓ.23 donation: 寄付　ℓ.26 on one's behalf: 〜のために

問1 下線部を日本語に訳しましょう。

_____

_____

_____

問2 フスト大聖堂を建設した人物について日本語でまとめましょう。

_____

_____

_____

問3 フスト大聖堂の特徴について日本語でまとめましょう。

_____

_____

_____

問4 1 ～ 5の英文が本文の内容と一致していれば **T** を、そうでなければ **F** を○で囲みましょう。

1. Church construction experts designed this cathedral.　　　　(T or F)

2. Justo completed the work entirely with his own funds.　　　　(T or F)

3. Most of the materials used in the building were not new.　　　　(T or F)

4. Justo once worked in a Trappist monastery.　　　　(T or F)

5. The construction of the cathedral ended with Justo's death.　　　　(T or F)

名詞と冠詞

Grammar Check

次の英文を見てみましょう。

> The grocery is famous for its friendly atmosphere. Ken runs it with his family. It sells dairy products, bread, meat, vegetables, water, and other foodstuffs.

名詞 (noun)

人や事物の名前を表す語です。

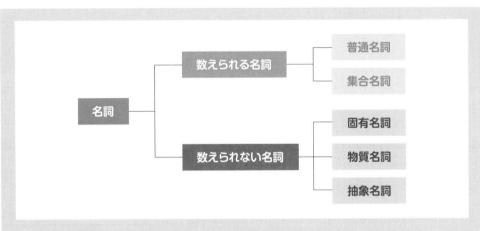

1　名詞の分類法

数えられる名詞……冠詞またはそれに代わる語や複数表示が必要

The grocery その食料品店、**Ken's** family ケンの家族、dairy product**s** 乳製品類、vegetable**s** 野菜類、foodstuff**s** 諸々の食材

数えられない名詞……複数形×、分量表現に工夫が必要

Ken ケン、water 水、bread パン

ex. 二切れのパン two pieces (slices) of bread

＊意味によってどちらにもなる場合があります。

There are 20 rooms in this inn. /

There is no room for doubt about his guilt.

🔵 冠詞 (Article)

形容詞の一種で、以下の2種類があります。

> 不定冠詞　a, an　＊one が変化してできたもの
> (a)「1つの」 I have a motorbike.
> (b) 種類一般を指す　A cat is an elusive animal.
> (c)「〜につき」I study math six hours a week.
>
> 定冠詞　the　＊that が変化してできたもの
> (a) 既出の語を指す　I have a motorbike. The motorbike is black.
> (b) 最上級を表す　My motorbike is the coolest in the world.
> (c) 唯一無二であることを示す　The sun rises in the east.

Applying Grammar

1 〜 6 の英文の下線部の名詞の種類を考えながら、日本語に訳しましょう。

1. Mr. and Ms. Smith will come to Japan next June.

   _____

2. All the crew were saved after the shipwreck.

   _____

3. A fire broke out in my neighborhood.

   _____

4. I'd like a glass of wine and a piece of bread.

   _____

5. His family are all well; the oldest member is his grandma.

   _____

6. Paris is the capital of France.

   _____

Understanding English in Conversation

Audio 09

次の会話を読んで問いに答えましょう。

Two women are talking in their dormitory on Saturday.

Paula: Hi, Ariana. I didn't expect to see you this morning. I thought you were going shopping for clothes.

Ariana: I already finished. I bought a new dress for my sister's wedding.

Paula: Wait! It's before noon. Did you have enough time to choose it? Were you even able to try it on?

Ariana: Yes, I used the "virtual fitting room" at a nearby store. It is just like a regular fitting room. But on the wall, instead of a mirror, there is a big computer screen. When I ☐ in front of it, a camera takes my picture and displays it on the screen. Then I select a dress on the touch screen, and the computer matches that dress to my virtual body. It can visualize how I look. Also, I can easily change the colors on the touch screen. Then, I just put on the one I liked the most, which fit me perfectly. I didn't have to try on any others, so it saved me a lot of time.

Paula: That's great. I'm going to give it a try, too.

Notes *ℓ*.8 virtual fitting room: バーチャル試着室　*ℓ*.12 touch screen: タッチパネル

18

問1 ☐ に入る最も適切な動詞を **1 ～ 4** の中から選びましょう。

1. cover

2. stand

3. offend

4. discover

答：☐

問2 本文中で使われている、数えられる名詞〔語 (a word)〕のすべてに下線を引きましょう。

問3 適切な答えを **A) ～ D)** の中から選びましょう。

1. アリアナが購入したのはどれですか？

   A) a present for Paula

   B) a costume for a play

   C) a formal party dress

   D) a new computer screen

2. 会話の内容として正しいものはどれですか？

   A) Paula tried the virtual fitting room.

   B) Both women will join the wedding ceremony.

   C) Ariana seems satisfied with her choice.

   D) Paula insists Ariana's new dress isn't good.

答： | **1** | | **2** | |

Understanding English through Reading

次の英文を読んで、問いに答えましょう。

Imagine you are at a party enjoying a few drinks. Late at night, you say goodbye to your friends, take your smartphone, and make a call. A taxi soon arrives to pick you up and take you home safely. After you get out, the car quickly leaves to pick up the next customer.

5　You don't even have to pay a tip because it's a self-driving car! AI-powered self-driving cars can drive at a safe speed. They are also designed to avoid collisions. Fuel consumption is also minimized because driving performance is smoother and more efficient.

Dreaming of such a future, various ⬚⬚⬚⬚⬚ worldwide

10　are designing and testing self-driving cars and improving their performance every day. As the system gets closer to reality, it will significantly impact developed countries like the United States.

In that country, for example, nearly four-fifths of drivers, or about 800 out of every 1,000, own their cars. In time, many people will

15　come to agree with the idea of sharing vehicles. This is because the increased availability of these shared vehicles will save time and energy, reduce driving stress, and protect the environment. The dramatic changes by automated shared vehicles will bring a global impact on how people move, how they think about transportation,

20　and how humans design future cities.

 ℓ.5 tip: チップ　ℓℓ.5-6 AI-powered: 人工知能搭載の　ℓ.7 collisions: 衝突　ℓ.7 fuel consumption: 燃料消費　ℓ.15 sharing vehicles: カー・シェア　ℓ.19 transportation: 輸送、運送

問1 ＿＿＿＿に入れる名詞として**不適切な語**を選択肢の中から選びましょう。

A) companies

B) manufacturers

C) developers

D) architects

答：＿＿＿＿

問2 下線部を日本語に訳しましょう。

_____

_____

問3 本文に登場する車両の将来的な利点とは何でしょう。日本語で答えましょう。

_____

_____

問4 1 〜 5の英文が本文の内容と一致していれば**T**を、そうでなければ**F**を○で囲みましょう。

1. Self-driving cars need extra fuel. (T or F)

2. Every self-driving car will cause traffic congestion. (T or F)

3. 80% of drivers in the United States have their own cars. (T or F)

4. Sharing a vehicle is much more costly than owning a car. (T or F)

5. Sharing driverless cars will change the future of city design. (T or F)

4 代名詞

Grammar Check

次の英文を見てみましょう。

> He loves his first shop because it gives him much pleasure. Who
> started it? Ken himself. It took him a long time to build the shop.

● 代名詞

名詞の代わりに用いられる語を「代名詞 (Pronoun)」といいます。
代名詞の種類には次の 5 つがあります。

1	人称代名詞	he, his, him, it
2	指示代名詞	this (that, these, those)
3	疑問代名詞	who (what, which)
4	関係代名詞	who (whose, whom, which, that, as, but)
5	不定代名詞	one, some, another (each, either, any, all, …)

人称代名詞の表　表を完成させましょう。

数	単	複	単	複	単	複	単 (所有代名詞)	複	単 (再帰代名詞)	複
格　人称	主 (は)		所有 (の)		目的 (を)		(〜のもの)		(〜自身)	
1	I	We	my		me		mine		myself	
2	You									
3	He									
	She									
	It									

It の用法

代名詞の It には様々な使い道があります。

> 時間、天候、距離などを表す、前出のものを指す、形式主語となる、など。
> Who started **it**?　**It** took a long time to do this.

Applying Grammar

1 ～ 3 の下線部の代名詞の種類を答え、4 ～ 6 の英文中の誤りを 1 箇所正しましょう。

1. It's too hot these days! Take care of yourself.

    It ⇒ 　　　　　　　these ⇒ 　　　　　　　yourself ⇒

2. This is the oldest coin that was found in the cave.

    This ⇒ 　　　　　　　that ⇒

3. What time do you get up every morning?

    What ⇒ 　　　　　　　you ⇒

4. Please lend me a pen or a pencil. Neither will do.

    _____

5. Those who do good thing for other will always be happy.

    _____

6. I have two cousins. One is a teacher, and another is a firefighter.

    _____

Understanding English in Conversation

次の会話を読んで問いに答えましょう。

Two graduate students are talking in their computer laboratory.

Shota: Helen, what are you doing? ①<u>You seem to be concentrating on your work.</u>

Helen: Oh, Shota. You surprised me! Yes, I'm working on my new
5　　　　software right now. Can you read this old Japanese book?

Shota: What is it? *The Tale of Genji*? No, I can't! The characters
look like snakes. ②<u>Maybe no Japanese students can read
such pre-modern characters these days.</u> Can you read
them?

10　**Helen:** 　　　　　　But now my new AI software will help me. I have
already installed thousands of variations of old Japanese
characters. Using this scanner, I highlight the word I want
to identify and the software reads it for me. This way,
anyone can read old documents.

15　**Shota:** That is exactly what Japanese need. It must have taken
you quite a long time. You should let other people know
about it.

Notes　*ℓ.6 The Tale of Genji*：『源氏物語』　*ℓ.10* software：コンピュータに命令を出すための
情報であるコンピュータ・プログラムのこと

24

問1 本文中で使われている人称代名詞すべてに下線を引きましょう。

問2 下線部を日本語に訳しましょう。

① _____

_____

② _____

_____

問3 適切な答を選択肢の中から選びましょう。

1. [　　　　] に入る適切な応答はどれですか？

A) I couldn't before.

B) Yes, of course.

C) Either you or I can do it.

2. 会話の内容として正しいものはどれですか？

A) Helen is learning ancient script from Shota.

B) Shota was not interested in Helen's plans at all.

C) They both have a hard time finishing their homework.

D) Helen used AI to make old characters readable.

答: | 1 |　　| 2 |　　|

Understanding English through Reading

Audio 13

次の英文を読んで、問いに答えましょう。

    If there had been no books in human history, our world would be very different from what it is today. Before 1440, there were only a few thousand books in Europe. They were very expensive and only a few people could afford them. But Johannes Gutenberg,
5 born in Germany about 600 years ago, took advantage of existing technologies to develop a movable-type printing press. His printing press was revolutionary in that it used movable pieces of metal and could print thousands of pages per day. However, Gutenberg did not achieve commercial success with this invention. Instead,
10 he gained lasting fame with the publication of the Bible.

    With the birth of the Gutenberg Bible, the Bible became accessible to ordinary people for the first time. <u>Gutenberg used his machine to print about 200 Bibles</u> on parchment and paper. Only about a quarter of these Bibles remain today, making them
15 extremely valuable. Gutenberg's printing press, the first of the three major inventions of the Renaissance, paved the way for mass transmission of information and had a profound impact on human society. It is said that Gutenberg continued to improve his printing press until he died in 1468. Although his tomb was destroyed by
20 later generations, he lives on today in the form of printed words.

 ℓ.4 Johannes Gutenberg: ヨハネス・グーテンベルク　ℓ.6 movable-type printing press: 活版印刷機　ℓ.13 parchment: 羊皮紙

問1 下線部を日本語に訳しましょう。

_____

_____

問2 グーテンベルク印刷機のどこが優れていると言っていますか？　日本語で答えましょう。

_____

_____

_____

問3 グーテンベルク聖書の特徴は何ですか？　日本語で答えましょう。

_____

_____

_____

問4 1 ～ 5の英文が本文の内容と一致していれば**T**を、そうでなければ**F**を○で囲みましょう。

1. Gutenberg became so famous that his tomb was rebuilt. (T or F)

2. Even before Gutenberg's invention, making books was possible. (T or F)

3. Gutenberg's printing press made him rich. (T or F)

4. Young Gutenberg invented the new printing press from scratch. (T or F)

5. People can see the Gutenberg Bibles, which exist even today. (T or F)

形容詞・比較

Grammar **Check**

次の英文を見てみましょう。

> Ken is an honest Japanese. He is two years junior to me. No one has a better personality than Ken. He has three little shops. The first one is made of wood and is the smallest; it's half as big as the others and Ken made it all by himself.

● 形容詞

「形容詞 (Adjective)」は基本的に 名詞を修飾 します。

1　形容詞は主に次のように分類されます。

A. 性状形容詞 (Qualifying Adjective)
　　記述　honest (old, big, kind, red) / 物質　wooden (metallic, stone)
　　固有　Japanese (American, Russian)

B. 数量形容詞 (Quantitative Adjective)
　　数詞　three (基数)，first (序数)，half (倍数) / much (不定数量)

2　形容詞の用法

(1) 限定用法　＊通常は名詞の前に置いて直接修飾します。
　　three (3つの) **little** (小さな) shops、**The** (その) **first** (最初の) **wooden** (木造の) one

(2) 叙述用法　動詞を隔て、文の補語となって間接的に名詞を修飾します。
　　Ken is **honest**. (ケンは正直だ。)

(3) The ＋ 形容詞→名詞
　　The strong should protect **the weak**. (強者は弱者を守るべし。)

(4) 前置詞 ＋ 形容詞→副詞
　　at **last** (ついに)、at **least** (少なくとも)、in **short** (つまり)

● 比較

形容詞や副詞には比較変化（Comparison）があり、2つ以上のものを比べる時に変化します。

1 比較を表す時は原級、比較級、最上級を用います。

A. 原級………2つのものが同じ程度である場合
The second shop is **as** big **as** the third one.
B. 比較級……2つの程度が異なる場合　The first shop is **smaller than** the second one.
C. 最上級……最も程度が強い場合　This is **the smallest** shop of all.
D. ラテン系比較級……**Ken is two years junior to me.**
＝ Ken is two years younger than I (am).

2 原級や比較級を用いて最上級の意味を表すことができます。

No other person has as good a personality as Ken's.
No one has a better personality than Ken.
Ken has the best personality of all.

Applying Grammar

 Audio 14

1～3の（　）内の選択肢から適切な語を選んで○で囲み、4～6の（　）内に入る正しい形を答えましょう。

1. This motorbike is the (latest, latter) fashion in Japan.

2. Light travels (much, very) faster than sound.

3. OK, do you have any (farther, further) questions about this?

4. Time is the (much) precious thing in life.

_____

5. She is one of the (great) scientists in the history of the world.

_____

6. This desktop computer is twice as (heavier) as that one.

_____

Understanding English in Conversation

次の会話を読んで問いに答えましょう。

Lui: Hey Siri, can you give me some information on the biggest statue in the world?

Siri: Okay. The Statue of Unity in India is the biggest statue in the world. It was completed in 2018 and it is 182 meters tall.

5 Saki: Lui, what are you doing? This is a place to study and read, not talk on your smartphone.

Lui: Oh, I'll put it on silent mode. Sorry. I was just looking up big statues and found the world's tallest statue as of now. But I can't picture how tall it is.

10 Saki: Let me see it. Oh, it's almost twice as tall as the Statue of Liberty in New York.

Lui: Oh, really? According to the site, this huge bronze statue honors Sardar Patel, one of the early leaders of India.

Saki: I know about him because I studied him in my history class.
15 He was called the "Iron Man of India." Before Patel, there were over 500 small states in India, each with its own leader. When India gained independence from the British, Patel united all these states together. He is remembered as the man who united India.

20 Lui: So people built the biggest statue to honor him.

Notes *ℓ.*1 Siri: シリ。自然言語処理を用いて質問に答える、Web サービス上のソフト名。 *ℓ.*8 as of now: 今 [現在] のところ *ℓ ℓ.*10–11 Statue of Liberty: 自由の女神像 *ℓ.*13 Sardar Patel: サルダール・パテール。インドの政治家、弁護士。ネルー初代首相の下で副首相・内務大臣を務めた。 *ℓ.*17 gain independence from: ～から独立する

30

適切な答を選択肢の中から選びましょう。

1. この会話が行われている場所はどこですか？

   A) In India.

   B) In a French restaurant.

   C) In the library.

   D) In New York.

2. ルイが銅像の大きさが分からないと言っているのはなぜですか？

   A) Lui doesn't understand Siri's English.

   B) Lui has never heard of that big statue.

   C) Saki can't explain how big it is.

   D) Because such a statue doesn't exist.

3. 会話の内容として正しくないのはどれですか？

   A) Siri asks Saki for help to answer Lui's question.

   B) The Statue of Liberty is half the size of the Indian Statue of Unity.

   C) Patel united small states as one nation.

   D) Siri said the biggest statue is in India.

   E) People built the Statue of Unity to honor Sardar Patel.

答：	1		2		3	

問2 下線部を No other で始まる別の比較級で表現しましょう。

_____

次の英文を読んで、問いに答えましょう。

前列左から4番目が中村哲医師（PMS・ペシャワール会提供）

Dr. Tetsu Nakamura loved insects. He got a chance to travel to the mountains between Afghanistan and Pakistan to search for them. While he was there, <u>many people asked him for medical treatment, and it was then he noticed that few hospitals had</u>

5 <u>enough medical supplies and equipment</u>. At that time, due to severe droughts and warfare, many people were suffering from malnourishment and diarrhea. In Afghanistan, there were very few places to find clean water. Dr. Nakamura gathered volunteers to help him dig wells to provide people with clean water. After

10 hundreds of wells had been dug, Dr. Nakamura decided to build canals to irrigate the dry land for crops. He drew inspiration from the canals built more than 200 years ago in Japan.

Back then, there were no machines to build canals, so villagers had to work together to construct them by hand. Dr. Nakamura

15 studied a lot about river management systems in the Chikugo River area in Kyushu. After several decades, the main canal about 24 kilometers long and many smaller canals started operation and the desert began turning green. Owing greatly to the canals and wells, many villagers returned home. Tragically, Dr. Nakamura

20 was shot and killed in December 2019. He became a star forever shining over the green land and the mountains he loved.

Notes *ℓ.6* drought: 干ばつ　*ℓ.6* warfare: 戦争（行為・状態）、抗戦状態　*ℓ.7* malnourishment: 栄養失調　*ℓ.7* diarrhea: 下痢　*ℓ.9* well: 井戸　*ℓ.11* canal: 運河　*ℓ.11* irrigate: 農地に水を引く　*ℓ.14* construct: 建設する

問1 形容詞を意識しつつ、下線部を日本語に訳しましょう。

_____

_____

問2 中村医師が井戸を掘ることを決意した理由は何ですか？　日本語で答えましょう。

_____

_____

問3 中村医師は治水事業の際、何を参考にしましたか？　日本語で答えましょう。

_____

_____

問4 中村医師とその事業に関し、**1 ～ 5**の英文が本文の内容と一致していれば**T**を、そうでなければ**F**を○で囲みましょう。

1. He went to the region because he was interested in insects. (T or F)

2. He wanted to open a hospital in Japan from an early age. (T or F)

3. He was passionate about providing clean water to Afghans. (T or F)

4. Eventually, these canals and wells turned the desert green. (T or F)

5. He gathered people to build a canal in Kyushu. (T or F)

Grammar **Check**

次の英文を見て、動詞と思われる語に下線を引きましょう。

Ken was poor when he came to New York. He got up early in the morning and worked all day. Now he goes to night school to study business administration. He will be a CEO of a food company someday.

● 動詞

文の中核をなす重要な品詞を動詞（Verb）といいます。主語に続く位置にあり、動詞（句）の把握が英文理解の鍵となります。動詞の位置が分かればその左側が主語（主部）なので、文の中心構造がつかめるのです。動詞の働きは複雑ですが、文中の働きに応じて以下のように複層的に捉えることができます。

1 be 動詞 vs. 一般動詞

　　be 動詞でないものは一般動詞です。まずは be 動詞の仲間たち 8 つを押さえましょう！

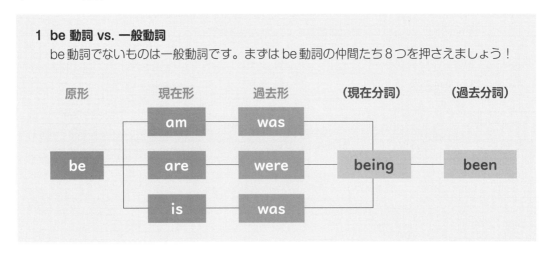

原形	現在形	過去形	（現在分詞）	（過去分詞）
	am	was		
be	are	were	being	been
	is	was		

2 一般動詞

疑問文、否定文には do, does, did / don't, doesn't, didn't がつきます。

＊「3（人称）単（数）現（在形）の s」の扱いについて理解が必要→goes

規則動詞	vs.	不規則動詞
ed のつく決まった変化形		独自の変化形

自動詞	vs.	他動詞
基本それ自身で使用できる		他者（対象・相手）を必要とする

定形動詞	vs.	不定形動詞（準動詞）
人称・数・時制により形が決まる		単独で使えず他の品詞の働きを兼ねる

本動詞	vs.	助動詞
文中で単独使用		単独使用不可。動詞の原形と共に用い、動詞を助ける

動作動詞	vs.	状態動詞
動きを伴う		持続的・静的←進行形にしない

単動詞	vs.	群動詞
単体		自動詞＋前置詞＝群動詞「他動詞」に等しい

Applying Grammar

1 ～ 6 の（　）内の選択肢から適切な語を選んで○で囲みましょう。

1. The student (rised, raised, rose) his right hand.

2. Please (lend, borrow, rent) me your smartphone.

3. What time did you (show, arrive, know) here?

4. Excuse me, what did that police officer (say, tell, talk) you?

5. My friend (lay, lied, laid) to me last night.

6. She (resembles, is resembling, look like) her grandmother.

Understanding English in Conversation

次の会話を読んで問いに答えましょう。

A: Hello! Welcome to the Space Science Exhibition Hall.

B: Wow, lots of people! May I have a brochure about the exhibition?

A: Yes, here you are. What are you interested in?

B: Space travel. Now, ordinary people are starting to go to space.

5　A: Yes, that's right. But space travel ☐ not just for tourism; it's also attracting much attention from a business point of view. For example, look at this panel. This private company plans to extract rare metals from asteroids.

B: Rare metals? Like platinum? Those are used in electronic
10　components, aren't they?

A: Exactly. There are limited resources on Earth right now. That's why there ☐ a movement to search for them in space.

B: We know that space ☐ still an endless frontier for humankind. But I hope that space will not be just a place to exploit, but
15　somewhere people young and old can visit whenever they want.

 ℓ.2 brochure: 無料案内図、パンフレット　*ℓ.8* extract: 抽出する　*ℓ.8* rare metal: レアメタル、希少金属　*ℓ.8* asteroid: 小惑星　*ℓ.9* platinum: プラチナ　*ℓ ℓ.9-10* electronic component: 電子部品類　*ℓ.14* exploit: (利益を得るために) 利用する

問1 この会話でのＡさんとＢさんの関係性は次のどれに当たりますか？

A) 引率教師と生徒

B) 部活の先輩と後輩

C) 案内人と訪問客

D) 岩石販売店員と通行人

答：◻

問2 次の問いに答えましょう。

1. 本文中で使われているすべての be 動詞に下線を引きましょう。

2. 本文中の ◻ に共通する be 動詞は何ですか？

答：◻

3. 会話の内容として正しいものはどれですか？

A) There are few visitors to this exhibition.

B) The visitor seems most interested in the results of space experiments.

C) Companies don't want to develop space resources.

D) Space travel is only for professional astronauts.

E) Space is seen as a source of rare metals.

答：◻

Understanding English through Reading

次の英文を読んで、問いに答えましょう。

A 170-carat pink diamond, the largest discovered in the last 300 years, was recently found in southern Africa. Diamonds [　　] among the most precious gemstones; their beauty has been appreciated for over 2,000 years. <u>Diamonds are not only beautiful but very hard.</u> Few materials are harder than diamonds. For this reason, most of the world's diamonds [　　] used in factories. They [　　] mainly used to polish camera lenses, break stones, and cut other diamonds. When diamonds were first discovered, people tried to find as many as possible. Diamond mining companies used heavy machinery to dig large holes in the ground, but they could not collect enough diamonds to meet the demand.

Scientists worked hard to figure out how diamonds are formed and to create artificial diamond stones, and they finally succeeded in 1954. Since then, scientists have concentrated on creating diamonds in the laboratory that closely resemble natural ones. Even experts cannot easily tell the difference between a diamond made in a laboratory and a natural one. It is now possible to create synthetic diamonds that are even harder than natural ones. However, people still seem to value natural stones more highly than synthetic diamonds. Interestingly, synthetic stones are used in only 2% of diamond jewelry.

 Notes *ℓ*.1 carat: カラット（ダイヤの重量単位）　*ℓ*.9 mining company: 採掘会社　*ℓ*.11 meet the demand: 需要を満たす　*ℓ*.18 synthetic: 人工の

問1 　□□□□ に入る共通のbe動詞はどれですか？

A) be

B) is

C) are

D) were

問2 　下線部を日本語に訳しましょう。

_____

_____

問3 　天然ダイヤと人工ダイヤの違いは何ですか？　日本語で答えましょう。

_____

_____

問4 　1 〜 5の英文が本文の内容と一致していればTを、そうでなければFを○で囲みましょう。

1. Natural diamonds can no longer be found on Earth. 　(T or F)

2. At first, mining companies could find lots of diamonds. 　(T or F)

3. Before the 1950s, synthetic diamonds did not exist. 　(T or F)

4. It isn't easy to distinguish between natural and synthetic diamonds.

　(T or F)

5. Synthetic diamonds are the most popular in the jewelry market. 　(T or F)

5文型と前置詞

Grammar Check

次の英文を見てみましょう。

> Anne grew up in New York. She was a college student when she met Ken in his shop. That day was her birthday, so Ken gave Anne a rose. The little gift made her happy for several days.

🔵 文の主要素

主語 S（Subject）、動詞 V（Verb）、目的語 O（Object）、補語 C（Complement）の4つを文の「主要素」といいます。

🔵 5文型

英文は述語動詞の性質によって5つの基本形（Five Sentence Patterns）に分かれます。

自動詞（Vi）
- I　第1文型（完全自動詞）　S+V
  Anne grew up in New York.
- II　第2文型（不完全自動詞）　S+V+C（S ＝ C）（C: 主格補語）
  She was a college student.

他動詞（Vt）
- III　第3文型（完全他動詞）　S+V+O（S ≠ O）
  Anne met Ken.
- IV　第4文型（授与動詞）　S+V+IO+DO（IO ＝間接目的語／DO ＝直接目的語）
  Ken gave Anne a rose.
- V　第5文型（不完全他動詞）　S+V+[O+C]（C: 目的（格）補語）
  The little gift made her happy.

前置詞

名詞（代名詞、名詞相当語句）の「前」に「置」く「詞（ことば）」を前置詞（Preposition）といいます。前置詞には、名詞・代名詞・名詞相当語句と、文中の他の語との関係を示す働きがあります。

文型を考える上でも前置詞は重要です。前置詞を含むそれ以降の語群（前置詞句）は文型において主要素とはならないことが多いからです。例　**in** his shop, **for** several days

---

＊前置詞から先は **M (Modifier) = 修飾語 (修飾句)** と考えることができます。

第3文型　He gave a rose to her. ←→ 第4文型　He gave her a rose.
　　　　　S　V　DO　M　　　　　　　　　　　　　　S　V　IO　DO

＊前置詞と同様に副詞・副詞句も修飾語 M で、主要素にはなりません。

Applying Grammar
🔊 Audio 20

1～3の（　）内の語句を並べ替えて英文を完成させ、4～5を正しい英文にしましょう。

1. The mother (daughter, a long e-mail, to, wrote, her).

2. You have (your, clean, to, keep, room).

3. The boss's (us, made, sleepy, speech, long).

4. We all know she is happiness after recovering from the disease.

_____

5. These flowers smell sweetly.

_____

Understanding English in Conversation

次の会話を読んで問いに答えましょう。

Duke: Have you ever heard the story of a junior high school student who built a robotic arm all by himself? He did it in a small rural town in Colorado.

Kana: No. How is that possible? I would think it would take a lot of preparation and funding.

Duke: Yes, but that's the truth. <u>The boy taught himself everything</u> he needed to know on the Internet. He bought a cheap 3D printer and built a mechanical arm for about $300. He was invited to the White House, where then President Obama shook the hand of the robotic arm.

Kana: That's amazing. So, is the boy still making robots today?

Duke: There was a turning point: when he exhibited the robotic arm at the 2012 Colorado Science Expo, he met a girl with a prosthetic arm. The girl's prosthetic arm was inferior to the robotic arm he had built and cost $80,000. So, he decided to make a better, less expensive prosthetic arm.

Kana: That's wonderful. One encounter changed his life. And did he achieve his goal?

Duke: ⬚⬚⬚⬚! He started his own company in 2014.

 ℓ.2 **all by oneself**: (仕事などを) 自分一人の力で、自分だけで ℓ.3 **rural**: 田舎の、地方の ℓ.13 **Science Expo**: 科学展示会 ℓ.14 **prosthetic**: 人工補装具の、義肢の ℓℓ.14-15 **(be) inferior to**: ～より劣っている ℓ.17 **encounter**: 出会い

問1 下線部は第何文型ですか？

答：[　　　　]

問2 適切な答を A) ～ D) の中から選びましょう。

1. 右の英文の後に続くのはどれですか？ Kana seems to be surprised because...

　A) Duke knows almost nothing about 3D printers.

　B) Duke's invention won a prize at the science contest.

　C) she tried to develop the machine, but she couldn't.

　D) a self-taught teenager made a complicated device.

2. [　　　　] に入る適切なものはどれですか？

　A) Yes, he did

　B) I don't know

　C) He must be the man

　D) He never did it

3. 会話の内容として正しいものはどれですか？

　A) The boy made a weapon for $300.

　B) The boy taught the girl how to make a prosthetic arm.

　C) The girl in Colorado asked him to build her a cheap 3D printer.

　D) The boy started a prosthetic arm company.

答： | 1 |　　| 2 |　　| 3 |　　|

Understanding English through Reading

Audio 22

次の英文を読んで、問いに答えましょう。

(A) Skin is the largest organ of the human body. The skin of an adult is about 1.6 square meters (the equivalent of one tatami mat) and weighs 3 kilograms, including subcutaneous tissue. On average, it is only 2 mm thick, yet it covers almost the entire body
5 and separates the inside of the body from the outside world. (B) It protects the body from external enemies such as bacteria, viruses, and UV rays. (C) Nature makes human skin a natural overcoat. It is waterproof and self-repairing, and new cells are constantly produced
10 in its lower layers. Older cells are pushed up to the outer layer to protect the body surface, and are gradually shed. Interestingly, this recycling of the skin usually repeats itself in 28 to 40 days, like the lunar cycle.

In recent years, scientists have advanced their dermatological
15 research and designed an artificial "e-skin" that can sense touch. This "e-skin" can respond to pressure at approximately the same rate as human skin. Eventually, scientists plan to connect the artificial skin to nerve cells in malfunctioning limbs to restore sensation. The "e-skin" will also be applied to robotics, and future
20 robots will be able to hold fragile objects such as wine glasses and eggs without breaking them.

Notes *ℓ*.1 organ: 器官　*ℓ*.3 subcutaneous tissue: 皮下組織　*ℓ*.4 yet: けれども、それにも
かかわらず　*ℓ*.6 external enemy: 外敵　*ℓ*.8 overcoat: 保護膜　*ℓℓ*.8-9 self-repairing:
自己修復性をもつ　*ℓ*.9 cell: 細胞　*ℓ*.13 lunar cycle:《天文》太陰周期、月の周期　*ℓ*.14
dermatological: 皮膚科学の　*ℓ*.15 sense: 感知する　*ℓ*.15 touch: 触覚　*ℓ*.18 nerve:
神経　*ℓ*.18 malfunctioning: 機能不全の　*ℓ*.18 limb: 手足　*ℓ*.19 robotics: ロボット工
学　*ℓ*.20 fragile: こわれやすい

問1 (A) ～ (C) の下線部を日本語に訳しましょう。

(A) _____

(B) _____

(C) _____

問2 人工皮膚の特徴は何ですか？ 日本語でまとめましょう。

_____

_____

_____

問3 1 ～ 5の英文が本文の内容と一致していれば T を、そうでなければ F を○で囲みましょう。

1. The skin has the least volume of a human organ.　　　(T or F)

2. Skin protects the human body despite its thinness.　　　(T or F)

3. Making artificial skin is impossible.　　　(T or F)

4. Human skin has already been implanted in many robots.　　　(T or F)

5. "E-skin" is expected to help restore lost sensations.　　　(T or F)

8 助動詞

Grammar **Check**

次の英文を見てみましょう。

> After the rose was given to Anne, she started dropping in at Ken's shop after school every day. Before long, she realized what a kind person he was. Now you can imagine what happened. They'll get married soon.

🔵 助動詞

他の動詞に付随して用いられ、それに特別な意味を付け加える働きを持つものを「助動詞（Auxiliary Verb）」といいます。

1 第1助動詞 (Primary auxiliary verb)
それ自体では意味を示しませんが、文法的に重要な働きを担っています。

① **be動詞**
現在分詞と一緒に「進行形」、過去分詞と一緒に「受け身」を作ります。
She **is** talking with Ken. / The rose **was** given to Anne.

② **have**
過去分詞と一緒に「完了形」を作ります。
Anne realized that Ken **had** been kind to everybody.

③ **do**
一般動詞の原形と一緒に「疑問文」「否定文」「強調」「倒置」を作ります。
Did Anne notice it?

2 法助動詞 ("Modal anxiliary verbs" もしくは "Helping verb")
本動詞が単独で表せない様々な意味を付加する働きを持っています。
Now you **can** imagine what happened. They**'ll** get married soon.

よく用いられるものは数が限られていますので、この機会にすべて攻略しましょう！

> **will (would)**［だろう、するつもりだ］，**can (could)**［できる、ありうる］，**may (might)**［してよい、かもしれない］，**must (had to)**［ねばならない、〜にちがいない］，**shall (should)**［だろう、べきだ］，**had better**［する方がいい］，**ought to**［すべきだ］，**need to**［〜する必要がある］，**used to**［よく〜したものだ］，**dare to**［あえて〜する］

3　法助動詞の「過去形」

　　would, could, might, should などは UNIT 14（⇒82 ページ）に出てくる「仮定法」の際に重要な役割を果たします。形としては「過去形」ではあるものの、現在の時制としても用いられる点に注意しましょう。仮定の意味を内包する**丁寧表現**として多用されます。

　　（例）Would (Could) you do me a favor?「恐れ入りますがご協力頂けますか？」

Applying Grammar

🔊 Audio 23

1 〜 6 の英文を助動詞に注意して日本語に訳しましょう。

1. You must not open the door to the cellar.

_____

2. The boy cannot play the piano.

_____

3. We'll be home at about 11:00 p.m.

_____

4. You ought not to sit up so late playing online games.

_____

5. He must read this letter. His mother wrote it.

_____

6. I would often play tennis with him.

_____

Understanding English in Conversation

次の会話を読んで問いに答えましょう。

Hina: Hi, Jane. Good morning.

Jane: Good morning, Hina! How was your first night in the dormitory?

5 Hina: To tell the truth, I ① ☐ sleep well because I heard you talking with someone.

Jane: Oh, I'm very sorry that I bothered you. I was talking to my AI robot parrot, Chatty.

10 Hina: (_____) It looks like a real bird. Please show me how to speak to it.

Jane: OK. Hi, Chatty, this is my new friend Hina. We share a room. Please tell her today's date.

Chatty: Hi, Hina. Nice to meet you. Today is February 4th, 2023.

15 Have a nice day.

Hina: That's amazing! Your robot parrot is communicating with us.

Hi, Chatty, ② ☐ you wake me up every morning at proper time?

20 Chatty: I'm sorry, Hina. I don't know your proper time.

Jane: Hina, you ③ ☐ give him a specific time, so he can understand what you mean.

Hina: I see. I think I will enjoy my new life with you and Chatty!

Notes ℓ.3 dormitory: 学生寮 ℓ.8 AI (Artificial Intelligence): 人工知能 ℓ.8 parrot: オウム
ℓ.9 Chatty: (鳥の名前)「お喋り君」 ℓ.21 specific: 具体的な

問1 ①～③ の ☐ に入る適切な助動詞を選びましょう。

1. could　　2. couldn't　　3. had better

4. ought not to　　5. used to

答： | ① | | ② | | ③ | |

問2 適切な答を A) ～ D) の中から選びましょう。

1. What are Jane and Hina talking about?

A) How to wake up Chatty.

B) How to share their daily lunch.

C) How to talk with the AI robot bird.

D) How to give food to Chatty.

2. （ ＿＿＿＿ ）に入る適切なものはどれですか？

A) Such a bird is difficult to keep.

B) Yes, I know the bird sings well.

C) I have the same robot, too.

D) Is this really a robot?

3. 会話の内容として正しいものはどれですか？

A) Jane wanted to talk to Hina at midnight.

B) Hina thought the bird wasn't real at all.

C) Chatty can't deal with unclear requests.

D) Hina is anxious about living with Jane.

答： | 1 | | 2 | | 3 | |

Understanding English through Reading

次の英文を読んで、問いに答えましょう。

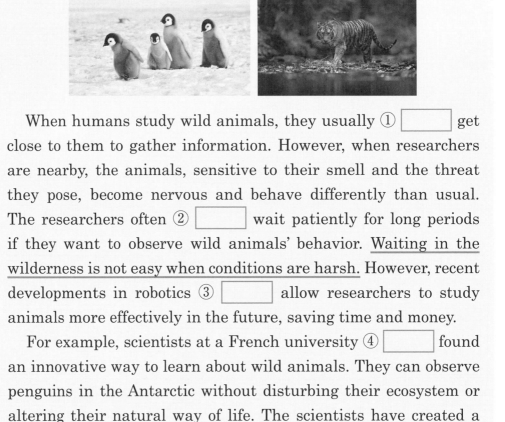

When humans study wild animals, they usually ① ▢ get close to them to gather information. However, when researchers are nearby, the animals, sensitive to their smell and the threat they pose, become nervous and behave differently than usual.

5　The researchers often ② ▢ wait patiently for long periods if they want to observe wild animals' behavior. <u>Waiting in the wilderness is not easy when conditions are harsh.</u> However, recent developments in robotics ③ ▢ allow researchers to study animals more effectively in the future, saving time and money.

10　For example, scientists at a French university ④ ▢ found an innovative way to learn about wild animals. They can observe penguins in the Antarctic without disturbing their ecosystem or altering their natural way of life. The scientists have created a robot penguin that looks and behaves exactly like a baby penguin.

15　Multiple cameras ⑤ ▢ installed inside this penguin-shaped robot, allowing researchers to observe the behavior of actual baby penguins. In addition, another camera is carefully hidden inside an artificial egg nearby. Using the robot and the spy camera in the egg, the team can gather about five times more information than

20　when using standard observation methods. In this way, the robotic penguins help study real penguins without stressing them.

Notes | *ℓ.7* harsh: 厳しい　*ℓ.11* innovative: 画期的な　*ℓ.12* the Antarctic: 南極大陸　*ℓ.12* disturb: 乱す　*ℓ.13* alter: 変える　*ℓ.14* exactly like: 〜にそっくりな

問1 ①〜⑤の [____] に入る適切な助動詞を選びましょう。1問につき正解は複数ある場合もあります。

1. will
2. must
3. are
4. have
5. need to
6. used to

答： ① [____] ② [____] ③ [____] ④ [____] ⑤ [____]

問2 下線部を日本語に訳しましょう。

_____

_____

問3 ロボット・ペンギンにはどのような利点があると言っていますか？　日本語で答えましょう。

_____

_____

問4 次の1〜5の英文が本文の内容と一致していればTを、そうでなければFを○で囲みましょう。

1. It is difficult to study wild animals in their natural state. (T or F)

2. The robot penguin could monitor the behavior of real penguins. (T or F)

3. Artificial eggs with cameras can be used as food for penguins. (T or F)

4. All penguins can identify robot penguins' smell and presence. (T or F)

5. The robots destroyed the penguins' natural environment. (T or F)

準動詞その1：分詞

Grammar Check

次の英文を見てみましょう。

> Look at Anne skipping down the main street! See, she's gone into Ken's store. Sitting in a chair with her eyes twinkling, Anne always talks about her day to Ken. Judging from the way she looks at him, she is obviously lovestruck.

準動詞

動詞から派生して出来た分詞・動名詞・不定詞を総称して「**準動詞（verbal, non-finite verb）**」といいます。**動詞的要素**があり、主語の人称、数、時制によって形が変わることはなく、単独で使うことができません。

分詞

分詞（Participle）には、元の動詞としての要素に「**形容詞**」**的働き**が加わります。「**現在分詞**」と「**過去分詞**」があります。

1 現在分詞
  動詞の原形に ing をつけた形。「〜している」という進行の意味を持っています。
  ① 限定用法
    ⅰ) 単独で修飾　the **skipping** girl（←名詞の前）
    ⅱ) 2語以上で修飾　Look at Anne **skipping** down the main street.（←後置修飾）
  ② 叙述用法
    第Ⅱ文型（S+V+C）や 第Ⅴ文型（S+V+O+C）の C（補語）の部分に置きます。

動詞の変化形の３つ目 (go-went-**gone**) にくるもの。受け身や完了の意味があります。

① **限定用法**
普通の形容詞と同様に、修飾する名詞の前後に置きます。
i)　単独で修飾　the **open-minded** girl（←名詞の前）
ii)　２語以上で修飾 The girl **open-minded to new ideas** is my sister.（←後置修飾）
② **叙述用法**
第Ⅱ文型（S+V+C）や第Ⅴ文型（S+V+O+C）のC（補語）の部分に置きます。
She is **open-minded**. / The father raised his daughter to be **open-minded**.

分詞を用いた慣用表現

Generally (Frankly, Strictly) speaking, Judging from ～ , Considering ～
一般的に（率直に、厳密に）言うと、～から判断すると、～を考慮すると

Applying Grammar

 Audio 26

１～５の（　）内の選択肢から適切な語を選んで○で囲みましょう。

1. That serial drama was very (boring, bores, boredom, bored).
2. These are drones (importing, important, imported, export) from Europe.
3. The writer spent half her life (wrote, writes, writing, written) this book.
4. Can't you smell something (burn, burned, burning, burns)?
5. We felt so (excite, exciting, excited, exact) that we couldn't sleep at all.

Understanding English in Conversation

次の会話を読んで問いに答えましょう。

🔊 Audio 27

Sakura: Hello, Yuta. I saw you ⬚drive⬚ a white car near the school parking lot yesterday.

Yuta: Yes, it's mine. I used to borrow my sister's blue sedan, but she needs it. So, I saved up my part-time job money and
5   finally got a small car last week.

Sakura: Good for you. Congratulations! But... you don't look so happy. And you missed yesterday's first class, right?

Yuta: Yeah, I was ⬚catch⬚ in a traffic jam and was late by two hours. There was a car accident and the main road was
10   closed.

Sakura: That was unfortunate. Anyway, you had better tell Professor Sato why you were late.

Yuta: I told him at lunchtime, but he just said I should have ⬚leave⬚ home earlier. I was moving slower than a pedestrian
15   when I went down the street. I wanted my car to fly!

Sakura: Flying cars have already been invented. They can take off and land vertically, requiring no runway.

Yuta: But I heard that at most, they can only fly for 15 minutes. That's not very useful, is it?

20 **Sakura:** But, in a few years, they may fill the skies.

Yuta: In any case, I will be a working adult by then. I hope my salary will be enough to buy one.

Notes *ℓ*.2 lot:（ある用途の）土地、場所 Ex. parking lot: 駐車場　*ℓ*.3 sedan: セダン型乗用車　*ℓ*.8 traffic jam: 交通渋滞　*ℓ*.14 pedestrian: 歩行者　*ℓ*.17 vertically: 垂直に　*ℓ*.17 runway: 滑走路　*ℓ*.21 by then: その時までに、その頃には

問1 ┌─────┐内の動詞を正しい形にしましょう。
     └─────┘

(drive) → _____ (catch) → _____ (leave) → _____

問2 指示文に従って答えましょう。

1. ユウタが冴えない表情である理由はどれですか？

   A) He lost all his money on the way to school.
   B) He was not able to attend yesterday's first class.
   C) Professor Sato was absent when Yuta visited his office.
   D) Sakura advises him to buy a new car.

2. 下線部を日本語に訳しましょう。

   _____

3. 会話の内容として正しいものはどれですか？

   A) Sakura is dissatisfied with Professor Sato's attitude to Yuta.
   B) Sakura doesn't know that Yuta was late yesterday.
   C) Both of them know about flying cars.
   D) Yuta likes his blue car and has no interest in changing it.

答： | 1 | | 3 | |

Understanding English through Reading

次の英文を読んで、問いに答えましょう。

Human transportation has evolved dramatically over time, beginning with the use of horses and camels. The invention of the wheel over 5,000 years ago opened up new possibilities. The wheel led to the animal-drawn cart, the bicycle, and the car—modes of
5 transport we still use today.

The steam engine, invented in the 1700s, is another important event in the history of human transportation. Steam locomotives, steamships, and steam automobiles propelled people forward by mechanical means. The Wright Brothers flew the first airplane
10 in 1903, the jet engine was invented in 1919, and within a few decades, air travel became accessible to millions.

But these advances have not come without problems, such as traffic accidents, congestion, and pollution. Cars and airplanes that consume fuels release greenhouse gases into the atmosphere,
15 which contributes to global warming. To tackle this issue, steps are being taken including the development of electric vehicles and introduction of biojet fuel. But if humans want to move around easily while living on a healthy planet, the evolution of human transportation needs to continue.

 ℓ.1 transportation: 移動 [手段] ℓ.9 mean: 手段 ℓ.9 Wright Brothers: ウィルバー とオーヴィルのライト兄弟。アメリカ合衆国出身、動力飛行機を発明した。

問1 下線部を日本語に訳しましょう。

_____

_____

問2 1700年代に起こった大きな交通上の変化はどのようなものでしたか？

_____

_____

問3 航空機の歴史的変遷についてまとめましょう。

_____

_____

問4 1～5の英文が本文の内容と一致していれば **T** を、そうでなければ **F** を○で囲みましょう。

1. People used camels for transportation in the early days.　　(T or F)

2. Inventions that have existed for over 50 centuries are still in use.　(T or F)

3. The Wright brothers' airplane flew in the early 19th century.　(T or F)

4. Human efforts to reduce fossil fuel emissions are important.　(T or F)

5. Humans should pursue only convenience and comfort.　　(T or F)

UNIT 10

準動詞その2：不定詞

Grammar **Check**

次の英文を見てみましょう。

It is a great pleasure for me to see Anne and Ken getting along so well. One day, Anne wanted to discuss something with me, so we went to dinner together. At the end of the meal, I saw Ken come directly toward us, just as Anne was kissing me on my cheek. In a quiet voice, Ken told Anne not to touch me. Needless to say, we had nothing to hide!

● 不定詞

不定詞（Infinitive）には元の動詞としての要素に「**名詞**」・「**形容詞**」・「**副詞**」**としての働き**が加わります。「**原形不定詞**」と「**to ＋ 原形（to 不定詞）**」の2種類があります。

1 原形不定詞
 to を付けずに動詞の原形のみを用いる特別な形です。

 I will **go.**　助動詞の後に使われます。
 I saw Ken **come** directly to us.　*S+V+O+C の補語の部分に使われます。

2 to 不定詞
 3つの用法があります。

 ① **名詞としての用法**「～すること」　a. 主語、b. 補語、c. 目的語になります。
 　　a. **To cook dinner every day** is a hard task.
 　　b. My grandma's ambition is **to go to Europe**.
 　　c. Anne wanted **to discuss** something with me.
 ② **形容詞としての用法**「～するための」「～すべき」　名詞のすぐ後について後ろから修飾します。
 　　We have nothing **to hide**!

③ **副詞としての用法**「〜するために」「〜するとは」「〜して」 目的、原因、理由、結果などを表します。

We went **to dinner** together.

He must be tired **to behave** like that.

All of us were shocked **to hear** the bad news.

3 to 不定詞の否定

不定詞の否定形は＜ not to 〜＞になります。

In a quiet voice, Ken told Anne **not to touch** me.

4 独立不定詞

文中の他の部分から独立して文全体を修飾します。

Needless to say（言うまでもないことだが）、to be frank（率直に言うが）、
to be sure（確かに）、to tell the truth（本当の事を言うと、実は）、
to say nothing of〜（〜のことは言うまでもなく）、等

5 It 〜 to 構文

形式主語 It を先に、真主語となる to 不定詞を後に置くことがあります。
英文は長い主部を避ける傾向にあるからです。＊意味上の主語は for+ 人で表します。

It is a great pleasure **for me to see** Anne and Ken getting along so well.

Applying **Grammar**

 Audio 29

1 〜 5 の（ ）内の語句を並べ替えて英文を完成させましょう。

1. My mentor (me, to, told, how, do) the difficult task.

2. People (win, would, to, like, him) the final match.

3. All (are, show, passengers, to, required) their tickets.

4. He (pay, back, promised, to, me) all the money.

5. It was (for, become, me, difficult, to) a professional tennis player.

Understanding English in Conversation

次の会話を読んで問いに答えましょう。

Aoi: Now it's time ① <u>to enjoy</u> the quiz! Who was the first Hispanic to go into space?

Asuka: I don't know. But you look excited. Was it a woman?

Aoi: Bingo! Ms. Ellen Ochoa. In 1993, she served on the nine-day mission of the space shuttle Discovery, the first shuttle to dock at the International Space Station. <u>She has spent about 1,000 hours in space and carried out many tasks.</u>

© NASA

Asuka: Did she want ② <u>to be</u> an astronaut from the start of her career?

Aoi: No, she started as a scientist. She studied physics and electronics and later specialized in optical systems for information processing. She has been active in space and on the ground and finally became the director of the Johnson Space Center.

Asuka: Wow! She is a real <u>all-rounder</u>. Incredible! It sounds like she has other talents.

Aoi: Good guess! She plays the flute well enough to be in an orchestra. She took it with her ③ <u>to play</u> in orbit.

Asuka: It's romantic ④ <u>to think of</u> her scientific and musical talents docking in space.

Notes *ℓ*.1 Hispanic: ラテンアメリカ（系）の人、（米国にいる）スペイン語を話す人　*ℓ*.4 Bingo: 正解　*ℓ*.6 dock:〔他動詞〕（2つ以上の宇宙船）をドッキングさせる　*ℓ*.8 astronaut:（特に米国の）宇宙飛行士　*ℓ*.10 physics: 物理学　*ℓ*.11 electronics: 電子工学　*ℓ*.11 optical: 光学の　*ℓ*.12 information processing: 情報処理　*ℓ*.13 director: 所長　*ℓ*.20 dock:〔自動詞〕ドッキングする

問1 ①〜④は to 不定詞の何用法ですか？

① _____ ② _____ ③ _____ ④ _____

問2 指示文に従って答えましょう。

1. 下線部を日本語に訳しましょう。

_____

_____

2. 〜〜〜〜線部分を別の語で表現するとどれに近いですか？

A) multi-talented   B) punctual   C) incompetent   D) unconscious

3. エレン・オチョア氏について、正しい記述はどれですか？

A) All she wanted was to be the first female scientist.

B) She took a key position at the Johnson Space Center.

C) In the end, she chose to be a music and art director.

D) She was born in 1993.

答： | 2 | | 3 | |

Understanding English through Reading

次の英文を読んで、問いに答えましょう。

© Everett Collection/shutterstock.com

Do you know the story of the most famous woman to sit in the cockpit of an aircraft? Amelia Earhart was born in a small town in Kansas on July 24, 1897 and spent her childhood in the countryside. Amelia was adventurous from an early age. At the age of seven,

5 she made a homemade roller coaster out of a wooden box and rode it off a roof. After she crash-landed, she said excitedly, "It was like flying!" <u>When she flew in an aircraft for the first time, she made up her mind about the future.</u> She took lessons at an airfield in Los Angeles to ⬚ her pilot's license.

10 While working various side jobs, including driving a truck, Earhart became the first woman to fly across the Atlantic as part of a three-person team and later set multiple aviation records as a solo pilot. She then utilized her brilliant career to become an ardent activist for women's rights and empowerment. However,

15 in 1937, during a round-the-world flight, Earhart and her co-pilot disappeared over the Pacific Ocean near the equator. In 1939, her death was legally recognized, although no evidence of a crash was found. Rumors therefore lingered for a long time that she was still alive. She is forever remembered as one of the world's pioneering

20 aviators.

 ℓ.2 aircraft: 航空機◆飛行機、ヘリコプター、グライダー、飛行船など、空中を飛ぶことのできる機体の総称。 *ℓ.5* roller coaster: ジェット［ローラー］コースター *ℓ.8* airfield: 飛行訓練場 *ℓ.13* utilize: 生かす、役立たせる *ℓ.14* ardent: 熱心な *ℓ.16* equator: 赤道 *ℓ.18* linger: いつまでも残る *ℓ.20* aviator: 飛行家

問1 ☐ に入る適切な語を選びましょう。

A) ruin

B) remake

C) cooperate

D) obtain

答：☐

問2 下線部を日本語に訳しましょう。

_____

_____

問3 イアハート氏はなぜ航空史において伝説的な存在となったのですか？　日本語で答えましょう。

_____

_____

問4 1 ～ 5の英文が本文の内容と一致していれば**T**を、そうでなければ**F**を○で囲みましょう。

1. Born in a big city, she obtained her pilot's license there. 　(T or F)

2. Earhart was active and adventurous from when she was a girl. 　(T or F)

3. At the beginning of her career, she was not a full-time pilot. 　(T or F)

4. Earhart was keen to improve the status of women. 　(T or F)

5. After her final flight in 1937, she lived happily in Kansas. 　(T or F)

UNIT 11 準動詞その3：動名詞

Grammar Check

次の英文を見て、動名詞と思われる語に下線を引きましょう。

> Anne was furious with Ken. It began raining and Ken left without saying another word. I insisted on her going after him, but she refused, so I stopped trying to persuade her.

動名詞＜〜ing＞

動名詞（Gerund）には、「名詞」としての働きが加わり、主語、補語、目的語になります。

1 他の準動詞との違いを以下の点に注意して比較して見てみましょう。

Point 1 「to不定詞」の「名詞としての用法＝〜すること」

i) 同じ意味で使えます。It began **raining**. = It began to rain.

ii) 全く意味が異なります。I stopped persuading her. / I stopped to persuade her.
動名詞→過去志向「〜（説得）していたのをやめた」
to不定詞→未来志向「〜（説得）しようとして（立ち）止まった」

iii) ① 動名詞、あるいは、② to不定詞を目的語とする場合があります。
① 動名詞を目的語とする動詞
mind, enjoy, give up, admit, avoid, finish, escape, practice, stop
postpone, deny, miss
② to不定詞を目的語とする動詞
refuse, agree, decide, desire, expect, hope, mean, offer, promise, wish

Point 2 「現在分詞＜〜ing＞」形は同じですが異なる働きをします。

i) The clown walked away singing. 道化師は「歌いながら」立ち去った。
→現在分詞「進行形（〜しながら）」

ii) Ken left without **saying** more. ケンは「それ以上何も言わずに」去った。
＊動名詞は前置詞の後に「名詞」として置かれるのです。

2　動名詞の意味上の主語

動名詞の前に名詞や代名詞の所有格や目的格を置いて意味上の主語を表します。

> I insisted on **her going** after him.

3　動名詞が完了形となる場合

Having (having) は、その前後の動詞との時間差を示します。

> I regretted **having** been involved in this.

4　動名詞を使った慣用表現

> I'm looking forward to **seeing** you tomorrow.
> It is no use **asking** her for help.
> How about **having** dinner here?

Applying Grammar

 Audio 32

1 ～ 6 の（　）内に入る正しい形を答えましょう。

1. Not (know) what to say, I remained silent to hear the sad news.

2. My brother was sitting in the chair with his legs (cross).

3. He is proud of having (be) a member of the Yankees ten years ago.

4. I remember (meet) Ken at that restaurant on the day it rained.

5. This book about pandemics is worth (read).

6. We can't help (admire) his attitude in helping the victims.

答：

	1		2		3	
	4		5		6	

Understanding English in Conversation

次の会話を読んで問いに答えましょう。

Moe: Mom, what do you want to do when you stop ① (work)?

Mother: After my retirement…15 years from now? Well, there must
5 be many things to do—taking care of Grandma and Grandpa, paying the mortgage, fixing up this house. And….

Moe: No, no, please don't get too realistic. Just tell me your dream!

10 Mother: Without ② (worry) about anything? Well, then, I like swimming, cycling, and taking photos. So I want ③ (live) on a southern resort island.

Moe: Having a dream is important, and it is the first step to getting what you want. And where do you want to stay on
15 the island? A small house ④ (face) the sea?

Mother: Now I understand what you are thinking about. Are you going to build something for me after you become an architect?

Moe: That's right! Look! I found an interesting article in my
20 textbook. A company developed a house that can be ⑤ (build) in a day. It is made mainly of paper and can be used as an evacuation shelter.

Mother: How kind of you! I'm sure you're going to be a good
_____ . Please add an entrance hall, a bedroom, a
25 bathroom, a make-up room, and my own exercise room.

Moe: Come on, Mom! Be more realistic! [laughs] A simple life would be the best for your dream island!

 Notes ℓ.7 mortgage: 住宅ローン　ℓ.22 evacuation shelter: 震災時避難所

問1 ①〜⑤の（　　　）内の動詞を適切な形にしましょう。

① _____　　② _____　　③ _____　　④ _____　　⑤ _____

問2 指示文に従って答えましょう。

1. 下線部を日本語に訳しましょう。

_____

_____

2. [　　　　　] に入る最適な語を選びましょう。

A) house designer

B) gardener

C) investor

D) housekeeper

3. 会話の内容として正しい記述はどれですか？

A) Mother and daughter are considering renovations.

B) Mother wants to keep working until she dies.

C) Moe is interested in a new style of architecture.

D) Mother is going to build a villa on an island.

E) Moe proposes to her mother to have a large second house.

答： | **2** | | **3** | |

Understanding English through Reading

次の英文を読んで、問いに答えましょう。

PLH-K- © Takanobu Sakuma

　Among famous Japanese architects active around the world, Mr. Shigeru Ban stands out. Fascinated by buildings he saw in architecture magazines, Mr. Ban moved to the United States as a young man to study architecture. Since then, based in Tokyo,
5　Paris, and New York, he has worked on large-scale projects, including museums, winning many international awards. One of the outstanding features of his architecture is his use of paper tubes as a building material.

　In addition to prestige projects, Mr. Ban has pursued an interest
10　in ＿＿＿＿＿ emergency shelters for refugees and victims of natural disasters. He has also established a volunteer organization to build temporary housing. He proposes setting up factories in developing countries to make shelters in preparation for disasters. These temporary structures can also be used to improve living conditions
15　in deprived areas.

　His idea has three crucial points: first, provide shelters immediately after a disaster; second, create job opportunities; and third, supply better housing in developing countries. The world needs more people like Mr. Ban.

 ℓ.5 large-scale: 〔活動・計画などが〕大規模の　*ℓ*.8 tube: 管　*ℓ*.8 building material: 建築資材　*ℓ*.9 prestige: 評判の高い、威信をかけた　*ℓ*.12 temporary housing: 仮設住宅　*ℓ*.15 deprived: 貧しい、困窮している

68

問1 [　　　　　] に入る最適な語を選びましょう。

A) degrading

B) stopping

C) providing

D) retreating

答：[　　　　]

問2 下線部を日本語に訳しましょう。

_____

_____

問3 坂 茂氏の建築の特徴を日本語で答えましょう。

_____

_____

問4 1 ～ 5の英文が本文の内容と一致していれば **T** を、そうでなければ **F** を○で囲みましょう。

1. This architect was born and raised in the United States.　　(T or F)

2. Mr. Ban constructed buildings in different countries.　　(T or F)

3. The architect has helped disaster victims.　　(T or F)

4. He is famous for his work using paper materials.　　(T or F)

5. He suggests that people always prepare for disasters.　　(T or F)

UNIT 12　12の時制

Grammar Check

次の英文を見てみましょう。

> It's been 20 years since I met Anne. The first time I spoke to her,
> she turned her face away. Her mother was holding her, but Anne
> suddenly jumped down and tried to kick me. Even today, she is
> still that spirited little girl to me, and always will be.

● 時制

動詞の変化形で表される（当事者の）時間の感覚を「時制（Tense）」という言い方で表します。

基本3時制を中心として、進行・完了・完了進行の意味合い（aspect）が加わります。
動詞の変化の型（パターン）の違いについて正確に理解しましょう。

● 基本の時制変化

基本動詞 study（原形）を中心、即ち現在に据えて考えてみましょう。
動詞が助動詞や準動詞と合体し [＿＿＿＿＿] 内の部分が以下【3×4】の12種の変化をすることがわかります。

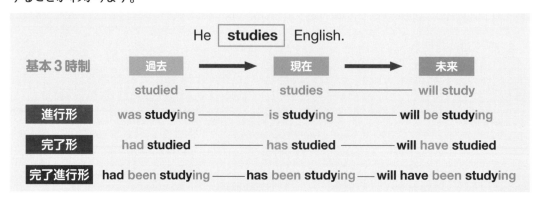

Point 1 基本3時制は時間的余裕を含みます。即ち、継続・反復・習慣などの行為や状態を示します。

He **visits** her on Sundays.
彼は日曜日に彼女の所へ行く。

She **is** still that spirited little girl, and always **will be**.
彼女は、今でもそうだが、これからも、あの元気な女の子のままでいつづけることだろう。

Point 2 進行形「(ちょうどその時) している、していた、しているだろう」ピンポイント感があります。

完了形「(ある時点まで) してきた、し終えた、したことがある」経験、結果、継続、完了を表します。

Point 3 完了進行形は Point 2 の「進行形と完了形」がミックスされた形です。

Applying Grammar

1 ～ 6 の英文の時制を正しい形にし、日本語に訳しましょう。

1. San Francisco is lying to the north of Los Angeles.

_____

2. The final tournament will be postponed if it will rain tomorrow.

_____

3. Water boil at a temperature of 100 degrees centigrade.

_____

4. Stan and Kitty were knowing each other since 2000.

_____

5. I was the last person to leave the lab. All other members would go home.

_____

6. His hotel, with 100 luxurious rooms, face the sea.

_____

Understanding English in Conversation

次の会話を読んで問いに答えましょう。

Hinata: ①You're rereading manga? You really love it!

Natsuki: It's my only distraction. Do you know Fujiko Fujio?

Hinata: Of course I do. Who doesn't know the creator of *Doraemon*?

Natsuki: This is an old work by one of them. ②I had a hard time getting hold of it.

5

Hinata: ☐ Does that mean there are several Fujiko Fujios? It's like a mystery.

Natsuki: ③ "Fujiko Fujio" actually refers to two cartoonists. Both are dead now. Fujimoto and Abiko worked together for over 35 years. The two were best friends since primary school.

10

Hinata: So, you mean two geniuses collaborated under one name to produce such great work? The apartment building they lived in became famous, right?

15 Natsuki: Yes, Tokiwa-so. ④Manga fans will never forget the name. Many other artists lived there and continued to inspire each other.

Hinata: How interesting! ⑤Will you have finished by noon? I want to read it, too.

 ℓ.2 distraction：気晴らし　*ℓ.2* Fujiko Fujio：藤子不二雄　*ℓ.9* Fujimoto and Abiko：藤本弘（ふじもとひろし）・安孫子素雄（あびこもとお）　*ℓ.15* Tokiwa-so：トキワ荘、漫画の「聖地」

①～⑤の英文の時制を答えましょう。

① _____   ② _____   ③ _____

④ _____   ⑤ _____

問2 指示文に従って答えましょう。

1. 〰〰〰 線部を日本語に訳しましょう。

_____

_____

2. [   ] に入る最適な英文はどれですか？

A) I know everything.

B) People always do so.

C) How about going out?

D) I don't understand.

3. 会話の内容として正しくない記述はどれですか？

A) Fujiko Fujio is the name shared by two cartoonists.

B) Hinata had no interest in that manga at all.

C) Natsuki was reading a vintage manga.

D) Fujimoto and Abiko worked together for a long time.

E) Tokiwa-so is associated with many artists.

答： **2** [   ] **3** [   ]

Understanding English through Reading

次の英文を読んで、問いに答えましょう。

Do you often read Japanese manga? Have you ever watched TV series with family or friends or watched anime at the cinema? Most people will answer "Yes!" But have you ever imagined how many people in the world watch manga "anime" every day? Japanese
5 animation has become very popular in the United States and other countries.

Doraemon, first broadcast in Japan in 1979, tells the story of a robot cat from the 22nd century who helps Nobita, a schoolboy. In the United Kingdom, for example, schoolchildren watched
10 this popular anime series in prime time . In fact, the anime has already been broadcast in more than 37 countries. Interestingly, apart from the language, the stories and characters have remained mostly the same. In Bolivia, where Spanish is spoken, Doraemon is called "Gato Cosmico" (space cat), and "Gyaian" is "Gigante" (giant child).

15 The internet has made it much easier for people all over the world to access Japanese culture. It is like having a real-life "Dokodemo-Door" (Door to Anywhere). As a result, interest in Japanese culture is growing worldwide and manga has played a significant role in this. You'll probably find fans of your favorite
20 manga in countries you don't expect.

 Notes *ℓ.7* broadcast:〔他動詞〕（番組を）放送する　*ℓℓ.11-12* apart from ~:～は別として、
～を除けば　*ℓℓ.12-13* remain the same: 同じ状態のままである、変更なしである

問1 [   ] の意味はどれに一番近いですか？

A) very early morning

B) midnight

C) at noon

D) a special hour

答：[   ]

問2 下線部を日本語に訳しましょう。

_____

_____

問3 海外で放送された「ドラえもん」はどういう特徴を持っていると言っていますか？
日本語で答えましょう。

_____

_____

_____

問4 1 ～ 5の英文が本文の内容と一致していれば**T**を、そうでなければ**F**を◯で囲み
ましょう。

1. Doraemon is the name of a robot cat from the 22nd century.　　(T or F)

2. The popularity of anime is limited to Japan.　　(T or F)

3. The anime characters are different in every country.　　(T or F)

4. Only people in Western countries are familiar with Doraemon.　　(T or F)

5. The internet has made it easier to watch animations abroad.　　(T or F)

言の葉を繋ぐもの

Grammar Check

次の英文を見てみましょう。

> Anne's biological father, who was a drunkard, had already disappeared by the time I met her. My father married her mother. After we started our new life, we became a real family. When our father died in a plane accident, Anne cried the most.

接続詞

語・句・節を結び合わせる語を「接続詞 (Conjunction)」といいます。

1　等位接続詞　and, but, or, for, nor
and の左右の語の品詞 (相当語句) を「等位」とみなすことが重要です。

My father **and** Anne's mother
He was a drunkard, **and** he had disappeared.

2　従位接続詞　after, when, if, because, while 等多数
節を用いて従属節とし、主節に従属させる働きがあります。

i)　名詞節を作る　I heard **that** Anne's biological father loved her very much.

ii)　形容詞節を作る　This is the reason **why** she first didn't like my father and me.

iii)　副詞節を作る　**After** we started our new life, we became a real family.

連結詞

関係代名詞、関係副詞、疑問詞は言葉を繋ぐ働きをするので「連結詞 (Connectives)」ともいいます。

1　関係代名詞　接続詞と代名詞の働きを兼ねます。
who-whose-whom, which-whose-which, that, what 等

Anne's biological <u>father</u>, [**who** was a drunkard], had disappeared.
⇒ 主節　Anne's biological father had disappeared.
　　従 (属) 節　who (=he) was a drunkard
　　アンの実父は、[酒飲みであったが] 失踪していた。

関係代名詞は [形容詞節] となって主文の名詞 (先行詞) を修飾します。
上の例のように間にコンマ (,) が入る場合は「非制限用法」といい、追加的情報となります。

2　関係副詞　接続詞と副詞の働きを兼ねます。
when (その時)，**where** (そこで)，**why** (それで)，**how** (このように)，**that**

When our father died in a plane accident, Anne cried the most.

関係副詞にも1の関係代名詞同様に、「非制限用法」があります。

They lived in New York, **where** Mother ran a small but famous restaurant.
彼女達はニューヨークに住んでいた。そこで母は小さいながらも有名なレストラン
を営んでいたのだ。

3　複合関係詞　関係代名詞や関係副詞に強意の -ever を付けた複合語です。
She welcomed **whoever** wanted to eat in it.
(=anyone who) 彼女はそこで食べたいと思う<u>人</u>は誰でも歓迎した。
Father would fly in from Boston **whenever** he had time to see them.
(=anytime when) 父は時間の許す<u>時</u>はいつでも彼女らに会うためボストンから飛び立った。

Applying **Grammar**　　🔊 Audio 38

1 ～ 6 の 2 文を 1 文にしましょう。

1. New York is a city. We have long wanted to visit.

　　_____

2. Have you found the documents? You lost them yesterday.

　　_____

3. Ken is going to marry the woman. You met her mother yesterday.

　　_____

4. The hospital is near Boston Common. Our father worked at the hospital.

　　_____

5. The airplane was hijacked. He was on board that airplane.

　　_____

6. The taxi driver was very kind. He took us to the airport.

　　_____

Understanding English in Conversation

次の会話を読んで問いに答えましょう。

Emi: Hey, what are you reading? A book about OOPARTS?

Bob: OOPARTS stands for "out-of-place artifacts." They are objects ① _____ seem to be too advanced for the technology of the time.

Emi: But don't they look [_____], as if they were made by a later generation?

Bob: You may think so, but some are being taken seriously by scientists ② _____ are doing research worldwide.

Emi: Give me an example.

Bob: Well, for example, this is the genuine OOPARTS ③ _____ devices were found on a ship wrecked near the Greek island of Antikythera over a 100 years ago. It's about 2,000 years old ④ _____ its construction is so complex that until recently, nobody knew ⑤ _____ it was. Would you like to read an explanation about it in this magazine?

Emi: Let's see. According to this article, it's a precision instrument with bronze gears. It is said to be an ancient Greek computer. How amazing! But what was it used for?

Bob: It was used as an astronomical calendar. Given that nothing like this appeared again until much later, it was certainly ahead of its time.

Notes *ℓ*.4 artifact(s): 工芸品　*ℓ*.14 genuine: 本物の　*ℓ*.15 wreck: (船) を難破させる　*ℓ*.16 Antikythera: アンティキティラ島　*ℓ*.20 precision: 精密　*ℓ*.21 bronze: 青銅の　*ℓ*.21 gear: 歯車　*ℓ*.23 astronomical: 天文の

問1 ①～⑤に入る語を下の選択肢から選びましょう。

① _____ ② _____ ③ _____ ④ _____ ⑤ _____

and	what	which	whose	who

問2 指示文に従って答えましょう。

1. 〰〰〰 線部を日本語に訳しましょう。

_____

_____

2. [＿＿＿＿＿] に入るのにふさわしくない語を選びましょう。

A) suspicious

B) doubtful

C) dubious

D) reliable

3. 会話の内容として正しい記述はどれですか？

A) The old device seems to have computer-like functions.

B) Antikythera is one of the Caribbean islands.

C) The students are consulting a 2,000-year-old book for research.

D) All OOPARTS are modern devices made by westerners.

E) Bob explains to Emi how to make OOPARTS with modern technology.

答： | **2** | | **3** | |

Understanding English through Reading

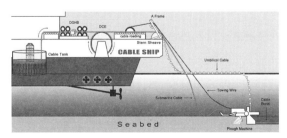

次の英文を読んで、問いに答えましょう。

There are probably more things in the ocean than anyone can imagine. Did you know that most data exchange between nations relies on submarine cables? These are cables laid on the seabed for ☐ between countries.

5　The first submarine cable was laid between Britain and France in August 1850 at great expense and labor, transmitting Morse code and other signals. Unfortunately, it was soon cut by the anchor of a fishing boat. After much trial and error, stronger cables were developed, and telephone and data communications became

10　possible.

Japan's first submarine cables connected Nagasaki to Shanghai and Nagasaki to Vladivostok in 1871, shortly after the start of the Meiji era. So, submarine cables have a long history. Building a network of cables presents many challenges. Cables can be

15　damaged by fishing vessels, sharks and other aquatic animals, and by earthquakes, tsunami, and underwater volcanic eruptions. They are vulnerable to attack in time of war and can also be a target for hacking.

Today, all continents except Antarctica are linked by nearly 500

20　thick cables. It is no exaggeration to say that telephone, internet and personal data communications, in other words, most of the world's communications, now depend on these submarine cables.

Notes ℓℓ.6-7 Morse code: モールス信号　ℓ.7 anchor:《海事》いかり　ℓ.12 Vladivostok: ウラジオストク　ℓ.13 the Meiji era: 明治時代　ℓ.15 aquatic: 水中に棲（す）む

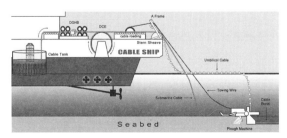

問1 [   ] に入る最適な語を選びましょう。

A) telegraph

B) satellite phone

C) communication

D) information war

答：[   ]

問2 下線部を日本語に訳しましょう。

_____

_____

問3 海底ケーブルにとっての障害とはどのようなものだったのでしょうか？　日本語で答えましょう。

_____

_____

問4 1 ～ 5 の英文が本文の内容と一致していれば **T** を、そうでなければ **F** を○で囲みましょう。

1. There is no longer anything to discover about oceans.　　　(T or F)

2. International information exchange relies on submarine cables.　(T or F)

3. Submarine cables are vulnerable to earthquakes.　　　(T or F)

4. Japan's first submarine cables were installed about 150 years ago.
　　　　　　　　　　　　　　　　　　　　　　　　　　(T or F)

5. Every continent except Antarctica is connected by submarine cables.
　　　　　　　　　　　　　　　　　　　　　　　　　　(T or F)

UNIT 14 仮定法

Grammar Check

次の英文を見てみましょう。

"Could you walk with me down the wedding aisle?" Anne asked me. "If I were older, I'd probably do it," I laughed. With a straight face, she said that I looked old enough to be a bride's father. I gave in and said yes. She broke into a radiant smile and jumped up, kissing my cheek. If Ken hadn't happened to walk in at that moment, he might never have seen us.

● 法

話者の心的態度を表すものを「法（Mood）」といい、下で述べる仮定法の他に次の2つがあります。

i) 「事実」として述べる直説法（Indicative Mood）　You walk with me.
ii) 動詞や否定辞を用いて「相手に命じる」命令法（Imperative Mood）　Walk with me.

● 仮定法

「仮定法（Subjunctive Mood）」は「事実」としてではなく、心中で「仮定」していることを動詞変化で表現する形態です。多くの場合、**助動詞の過去形が重要な働き**をします。

1　仮定法現在……「祈願・願望・要求・主張」を表します。
　i)　限定的に用いられます。　God **save** the King!
　ii)　that 節で原形を用いる場合があります。　We insisted that he **pay** the bill.
2.　仮定法過去……「現在」の話です。＊→の後の直説法と比較してどう違うかを確認しましょう。
　If I were older, I would do it. → I am not older, so I don't do it.

3. 仮定法過去完了……「過去」の話です。

   If our father had been alive, he would have done it.
     → As our father was dead, he couldn't do it.

   If Ken hadn't happened to walk in at that moment, he might never have seen us.
     → As Ken happened to walk in, he saw us.

Applying Grammar

 Audio 41

1 ～ 5の2つの英文がほぼ同じ意味になるように（　）内に適語を入れましょう。

1. I'm sorry I'm not in the concert hall now.

   I wish I (　　　　　　　　) in the concert hall now.

2. My grandparents didn't hurry, so they missed the train.

   If my grandparents (　　　　　　　) (　　　　　　　　　), they might have
   caught the train.

3. You didn't listen to my advice. Therefore you are in such trouble.

   If you (　　　　　　　) (　　　　　　　　) to my advice, you (　　　　　　　　)
   (　　　　　　　) be in such trouble.

4. "Why don't you give up smoking right now," my teacher said to me.

   My teacher suggested that (　　　　　　　) (　　　　　　　　) up smoking
   immediately.

5. But for his assistance, I could not have finished the job.

   If (　　　　　　　) (　　　　　　　　) not been for his assistance, I could not
   have finished the job.

Understanding English in Conversation

次の会話を読んで問いに答えましょう。

Allie: Your standby screen is unusual. Do you like the *Mona Lisa*? It looks scary if you see it at night.

Jun: ☐ What are you talking about? There is no one more beautiful than the woman in that painting. She is the symbol
5 of perfect beauty. It's as if she is looking at me from every angle of my cell phone. If only I knew what she was thinking.

Allie: It sounds like you think she is still alive. To me, she looks like a witch. The fact that she has been unharmed by ink, cake, and other attacks is also a mystery to me.

10 **Jun:** The Louvre exposes the *Mona Lisa* to the eyes of millions of people every year. If it were up to me, I'd hide her in a secure location where no one could come and see her.

Allie: Wow, that's so selfish! You really are obsessed with her.

Jun: Oh, if only I could see her in real life! Her mysterious smile is
15 what makes her so attractive.

Notes *ℓ*.1 standby screen: 待ち受け画面　*ℓ*.6 if only: ただ〜でさえあればいいのだが　*ℓ*.8 witch: 魔女　*ℓ*.8 unharmed by: 〜の攻撃を受けても無傷の　*ℓ*.10 the Louvre: ルーブル美術館　*ℓ*.11 secure: 安全な、厳重に警備された　*ℓ*.13 selfish: 自分勝手な　*ℓ*.13 (be) obsessed with: 〜で頭がいっぱいである、〜に夢中である

84

問1 下線部を日本語に訳しましょう。

_____

_____

問2 ☐ に入る最適な語を選びましょう。

A) Gorgeous!　　**B)** Frightening!　　**C)** Nonsense!　　**D)** Bingo!

問3 会話の内容として正しい記述は次のうちどれですか？

A) Jun feels the *Mona Lisa* is a little scary.

B) Jun understands everything about the woman.

C) The picture was attacked by a cake.

D) Mona Lisa is still alive as a witch.

E) A few hundred people come to see the picture every year.

答： | **2** | | **3** | |

Understanding English through Reading

 Audio 43

次の英文を読んで、問いに答えましょう。

Leonardo da Vinci painted one of the masterpieces of Renaissance art, the *Mona Lisa*. His name translates into English as "Leonardo from the town of Vinci." He was born on April 15, 1452 in a small Italian village, never married, and had no children.

5　There are many theories about the model for the *Mona Lisa*, but she has yet to be identified. However, it can be assumed that the portrait was 　　　　 to him, as he kept it throughout his life.

Da Vinci is the most famous genius of all time. He was not only an artist, but also a scientist and inventor. He loved animals,

10　especially birds. He studied the way birds flew and looked forward to the day when humans would be able to fly like real birds. When he died on May 2, 1519, he left behind more than 13,000 pages of notes and drawings. These include plans for hang gliders, helicopters,

15　and fighter planes. Amazingly, he made these sketches some 500 years before aircraft came into existence. Now he is known as the father of modern science. <u>What would he say</u>

20　<u>if he were alive today and could see</u> <u>these machines for himself?</u>

Notes　*ℓ*.1 masterpiece：傑作　*ℓℓ*.1-2 Renaissance：文芸復興期の、ルネサンスの

問1 ┌────────┐ に入る最適な語を選びましょう。

A) irreplaceable

B) boring

C) worthless

D) negative

答： ┌────────┐

問2 下線部を日本語に訳しましょう。

_____

_____

問3 ダ・ヴィンチは画家として以外にどんな才能を持っていましたか？　日本語で答えましょう。

_____

_____

問4 1 〜 5 の英文が本文の内容と一致していれば **T** を、そうでなければ **F** を○で囲みましょう。

1. Leonardo is the name of the painter's town.　(T or F)

2. Leonardo succeeded in making an actual helicopter.　(T or F)

3. The identity of the *Mona Lisa* model is still a mystery.　(T or F)

4. Leonardo died shortly after his 67th birthday.　(T or F)

5. Leonardo is known only as a great painter.　(T or F)

特殊構文

Grammar Check

次の英文を見てみましょう。

> Ken apologized for his misunderstanding. The incident made them much closer. At the party, Ken and Anne smiled happily at each other. I noticed an old man at the window. With tears in his eyes, he was staring at the couple.

🗨 倒置構文

S+V の基本語順が入れ替わる場合があります。

i)	Wh 疑問文，Yes-No 疑問文	Who on earth is he? / Is he crying?
ii)	There，Here で始まる	There was an old man. / Here comes your father!
iii)	仮定法で If を省略する	Were I Ken, I would let him in.
iv)	補語や目的語を強調する	**An old man** I noticed at the window.
v)	副詞語句が文頭にくる	**With tears in his eyes**, he was staring at the couple.

🗨 強調構文

強調する場合、色々な表現方法があります。

i)	do ＋動詞	**I do** hope Anne will not be angry.
ii)	It（be）〜 that...特定の文中の語句	**It was Anne's father that stood at the window.**
	*強調の場合、It（be）~ that を除いても文が成立します。	
iii)	再帰代名詞を用いる	**Ken himself**
iii)	副詞 very, ever, even などを用いる	He was **very** much like Anne.
iv)	反復	I saw him **again and again**.
v)	疑問形式	**Who in the world** believes such a thing!

否定文

「どの語、どの部分の否定」かについて見極めることが大事です。

否定文の作り方
   i)   be 動詞及び助動詞はその次に not, never を置きます。
   ii) 一般動詞は not, never を置きます。
   iii) 準否定語を用います。(ほとんど…ない)
       hardly, scarcely, barely……程度、seldom, rarely……頻度、few……数、little……量
       I could **barely** say a word.

部分否定と全体否定
   i)   部分否定……程度、not に both, all, every などが続くと「全部が〜ではない」
                 Not everyone recognized him, but Anne did.
   ii) 全体否定……not either, not any, no+名詞, none, neither で「誰も／何も〜ない」
                 None of us has done anything wrong.

否定を含む表現
   far from, anything but, by no means, not in the least (〜でない)、
   the last…to.. (決して〜しない)

Applying Grammar Audio 44

1 〜 6 の英文を日本語に訳しましょう。

1. There's no air-conditioning in any of these offices.

   _____

2. You're kidding me! He is no more a doctor than I am.

   _____

3. Little did the actress dream that she would win the prize.

   _____

4. On top of the hill stands the ancient castle.

   _____

5. What on earth do you want me to do?

   _____

6. "I'm thirsty!" — "So am I!"

   _____

Understanding English in Conversation

🔊 Audio 45

次の会話を読んで問いに答えましょう。

  Yuki: Taro, where were you yesterday? I came by to show you an alarm clock I made.

  Taro: Oh, sorry. I spent the night in hospital.

  Yuki: What? Why? Did you get hurt or sick or something?

5 **Taro:** [   ] Jun asked me to help him test his new bed sensor, so I played the role of a patient. The sensor monitors a patient's movements and sends data to the nurses' station. The data of patients' movements on the bed can be used to check their conditions and helps to reduce the nurses'

10   workload. If a patient leaves the bed, they will notice right away.

  Yuki: Oh, that's good to know. Sounds like exciting research. But could you sleep through the night? <u>I've never been in a hospital, so I can't imagine what it's like.</u>

15 **Taro:** Well, I slept too well for a few hours. But the sensor seemed to notice that I was motionless, so the nurses woke me up and told me to try moving a bit [laughs].

  Yuki: I see. So that's why you were so sleepy today and could barely stay awake during Professor Sato's class. Here, this

20   is my new alarm clock. Please use it if you want.

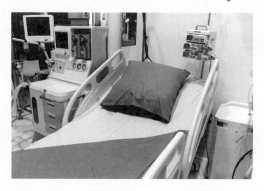

  ℓ.6 sensor: センサー (動きなどに反応する感知器) *ℓ*.10 workload: 仕事量、仕事の負担

問1 下線部を日本語に訳しましょう。

_____

_____

問2 ☐☐☐☐ に入る最適な応答を選びましょう。

A) Yes. It was a bad accident.

B) Nothing like that at all.

C) My mother was worried about me.

D) I thought you would come soon.

答： ☐☐☐☐

問3 会話の内容として正しい記述はどれですか？

A) Yuki visited Taro yesterday with the sensor.

B) Taro stayed in the hospital for a check-up.

C) Taro has invented the bed sensor.

D) The nurse showed Taro an alarm clock.

E) Taro was sleepy because of a lack of sleep.

答： ☐☐☐☐

Understanding English through Reading

次の英文を読んで、問いに答えましょう。

The novel coronavirus became a major global problem after it first appeared in late 2019. Remember the last time a deadly virus invaded the world? About 100 years ago, the three-year Spanish flu pandemic killed 400,000 people in Japan and at least
5 40 million worldwide between 1918 and 1920. But it was not from Spain that the Spanish flu spread. In the middle of World War I, millions of soldiers were fighting, and both sides wanted to hide the fact that an epidemic had broken out. Spain, then a neutral country, made information about the disease public. As a result, it
10 was misleadingly named the "Spanish flu," and many still believe it originated in Spain.

The Spanish flu and COVID-19 have several things in common. Both diseases were caused by viruses and quickly spread throughout the world. Governments were ill-prepared for them and responded
15 in a very ad-hoc manner. An outbreak of infection is likely to cause severe damage to society. Viruses, the invisible enemy of humans, are a constant ⬚.

Societies have fought and survived many infectious diseases, including the Spanish flu. The novel coronavirus will be no
20 exception. However, we must not forget that there are still many unknown viruses on our planet, nor should we neglect to take every possible precaution in our daily lives.

Notes *ℓ*.1 novel: （ウイルスなどが）新型の　*ℓ*.1 coronavirus: コロナウイルス　*ℓ*.4 pandemic: 大流行　*ℓ*.8 epidemic: 疫病　*ℓ*.8 break out: 〔急に・突然〕起こる　*ℓ*.8 neutral: 中立の　*ℓ*.10 misleadingly: 誤解を招きかねない　*ℓ*.12 COVID-19 = coronavirus disease 2019: 新型コロナウイルス感染症　*ℓ*.15 ad-hoc: 場当たり的な　*ℓ*.22 precaution: 予防策

問1 ☐ に入る最適な語を選びましょう。

A) curiosity

B) excitement

C) threat

D) support

答：☐

問2 下線部を日本語に訳しましょう。

_____

_____

問3 スペイン風邪の特徴はどのようなものですか？　日本語で答えましょう。

_____

_____

_____

_____

問4 1 ～ 5の英文が本文の内容と一致していれば**T**を、そうでなければ**F**を○で囲みましょう。

1. Spanish flu is not of Spanish origin.　　　　　　　　　　(T or F)

2. Infectious diseases have nothing in common.　　　　　　(T or F)

3. Humans have been fighting infectious diseases.　　　　　(T or F)

4. All governments were well-prepared for COVID-19.　　　　(T or F)

5. We need to take measures against viruses.　　　　　　　(T or F)

Words and Phrases Checklist

Adjectives

- ☐ **ad-hoc** …… 場当たり的な
- ☐ **ardent** …… 熱心な
- ☐ **astronomical** …… 天文の
- ☐ **fragile** …… こわれやすい
- ☐ **genuine** …… 本物の
- ☐ **harsh** …… 厳しい
- ☐ **innovative** …… 画期的な
- ☐ **neutral** …… 中立の
- ☐ **novel** …… （ウイルスなどが）新型の
- ☐ **optical** …… 光学の
- ☐ **prestige** …… 評判の高い、威信をかけた
- ☐ **prosthetic** …… 人工補装具の、義肢の
- ☐ **rural** …… 田舎の、地方の
- ☐ **secure** …… 安全な、厳重に警備された
- ☐ **selfish** …… 自分勝手な
- ☐ **specific** …… 具体的な
- ☐ **supersonic** …… 超音速の
- ☐ **synthetic** …… 人工の

Adverb

- ☐ **vertically** …… 垂直に

Nouns

- ☐ **astronaut** …… （特に米国の）宇宙飛行士
- ☐ **aviator** …… 飛行家
- ☐ **blueprint** …… 設計図
- ☐ **canal** …… 運河
- ☐ **collisions** …… 衝突
- ☐ **distraction** …… 気晴らし
- ☐ **donation** …… 寄付
- ☐ **drought** …… 干ばつ
- ☐ **electronics** …… 電子工学
- ☐ **encounter** …… 出会い
- ☐ **enigma** …… 謎
- ☐ **epidemic** …… 疫病
- ☐ **equator** …… 赤道
- ☐ **evacuation shelter** …… 震災時避難所
- ☐ **fuel consumption** …… 燃料消費
- ☐ **leakage** …… 漏洩（ろうえい）
- ☐ **limb** …… 手足
- ☐ **lot** …… （ある用途の）土地、場所
- ☐ **malnourishment** …… 栄養失調
- ☐ **masterpiece** …… 傑作
- ☐ **mean** …… 手段
- ☐ **mortgage** …… 住宅ローン

□ **pandemic** …… 大流行

□ **pedestrian** …… 歩行者

□ **physics** …… 物理学

□ **precaution** …… 予防策

□ **reconstruction** …… 再建

□ **runway** …… 滑走路

□ **sharing vehicles** …… カー・シェア

□ **standby screen** …… 待ち受け画面

□ **touch screen** …… タッチパネル

□ **transportation** …… 輸送、運送／移動 [手段]

□ **warfare** …… 戦争（行為・状態）、抗戦状態

□ **well** …… 井戸

□ **workload** …… 仕事量、仕事の負担

Phrases

□ **all by oneself** …… （仕事などを）自分一人の力で

□ **apart from ~** …… ～は別として

□ **as of now** …… 今 [現在] のところ

□ **break out** …… 〔急に・突然〕起こる

□ **by then** …… その時までに、その頃には

□ **if only** …… ただ～でさえあればいいのだが

□ **(be) inferior to** …… ～より劣っている

□ **make a detour** …… 寄り道をする

□ **meet the demand** …… 需要を満たす

□ **(be) obsessed with** …… ～に夢中である

□ **on one's behalf** …… ～のために

Verbs

□ **alter** …… 変える

□ **construct** …… 建設する

□ **disturb** …… 乱す

□ **exploit** …… （利益を得るために）利用する

□ **extract** …… 抽出する

□ **irrigate** …… 農地に水を引く

□ **linger** …… いつまでも残る

□ **utilize** …… 生かす、役立たせる

Photo Credit

Cover 　（最上段左から）© photravelerYUUKI/ shutterstock.com; © Hernan J. Martin/ shutterstock.com; © vladsilver/ shutterstock.com（中段左から）© J J Osuna Caballero/ shutterstock.com; PMS・ペシャワール会提供; © Pavel Vinnik/ shutterstock.com（最下段左から）PLH-K-© Takanobu Sakuma; © Everett Collection/ shutterstock.com

Stories of Pioneers:
Paths to Reading through Grammar

文法と読解の相互学習

2023 年 4 月 7 日　初版第 1 刷発行
2024 年 4 月 10日　初版第 2 刷発行

著　者　山田久美

発行者　森　信久
発行所　**株式会社　松 柏 社**
〒 102-0072　東京都千代田区飯田橋 1-6-1
TEL 03 (3230) 4813（代表）
FAX 03 (3230) 4857
http://www.shohakusha.com
e-mail: info@shohakusha.com

英語監修　　　　　　　　J&Y Works
本文レイアウト・組版　　株式会社インターブックス
装幀　　　　　　　　　　小島トシノブ（NONdesign）
印刷・製本　　　　　　　シナノ書籍印刷株式会社

ISBN978-4-88198-785-8
略号＝ 785